Ibn Ḥazm

on the lawfulness of women attending prayers in the mosque

Ibn Ḥazm

on the lawfulness of women attending prayers in the mosque

presented, translated, and annotated by
Mohammad Akram Nadwi

Interface Publications, Oxford
2018

Published in the United Kingdom by
Interface Publications Ltd. in association with Cambridge Islamic College

Interface Publications Ltd.
15 Rogers Street
Oxford. OX2 7JS
www.interfacepublications.com
tel: +44 (0)1865 510251

Cambridge Islamic College
58 Sturton Street
Cambridge. CB1 2QA
www.cambridgeislamiccollege.org
tel: +44 (0)1223 655223

First published: January 2015
2nd extended edition: March 2018

ISBN paperback: 978–1999872–0–6

A CIP data record is available from the British Library

Contents

Preface to the second edition

The argument of this book was first presented in a little pamphlet published in January 2015. Reactions to it were mostly positive. This is not surprising since, these days, any promotion of a women's 'right', of which men have allegedly deprived them, was bound to be a popular, easy read. To the original text (here reproduced with some minor corrections) I have appended further discussion. The core of this new material is responses to questions put to me that were critical. The matters raised in these criticisms are mostly dealt with in the translated text itself or in the notes, but I must accept that I did not do enough in the Introduction to spell things out as clearly as I ought to have done. In trying to correct that I do risk re-stating some of the argument. Let me begin this correction by re-stating the main issue more explicitly.

In some Muslim communities (notably in South Asia and other places, such as the United Kingdom, to which South Asian Muslims have emigrated), it has long been the custom that women do not (and think they are not supposed to) go to the mosques to do their prayers. As a result many people believe that this arrangement must have religious authority. How else could it have remained so well established – surely, in all this time, some scholar would have pointed to the error, if it truly were an error? When informed that in other Muslim communities, women do attend mosque prayers, albeit in numbers very much fewer than men, and not at all as regularly, they may well recognize that women are allowed to pray in the mosques.

It does not follow from that recognition that people long used to discouraging women from going to the mosques then change their practice. They change only the argument they use to support it. Instead of claiming that the religion commands women to pray at home, they now say that it is equally permissible that they pray at home or in the mosque. If they stopped there, no-one could object to it except that it is not what is *permissible* that is at issue, but what is *commended.* However, they go on to say: given the decline in standards of men and women's behaviour, it is better that women pray at home.

Thus, women going out to the mosques is not presented as an option equal to not doing so. Rather, that they pray at home or elsewhere not in public is explicitly presented as the *better* option, as what women *should* do. It follows that some communities feel neither duty nor need to provide facilities at the mosques for women. At the extreme this constitutes a tacit justification for refusing entry to women. This has happened at a number of mosques in the UK. For a believer to be turned away from a mosque is an affront so painful that most women are deterred from even thinking about challenging the practice. In short, even though people know and agree that it should not be so, discouraging women from doing their prayers in the mosque remains a well-established custom. My aim in writing this book is to make the argument of Ibn Ḥazm available in English so that people without access to the original become aware that this custom is contradictory to the *sunnah* of the Prophet, upon him be peace, and the practice of his Companions. Whether they are then willing and able to implement reform of that custom is a separate question.

As those who have heard me teach this subject will know, I describe *refusing* to allow women to attend prayers in the mosque (as distinct from *discouraging* their attendance) as *bidʿah*. The meaning of *bidʿah* in ordinary language is innovation, some thing or usage for which there is no precedent. It is quite appropriate to use the word for improvement or change in techniques (in how we build buildings, produce goods and services, travel, communicate, etc.) and life-styles and tastes that are not inhibited by religious considerations. However, *bidʿah* is also used as a technical term with a very particular meaning. It is used, in respect of the formulation of religious beliefs (the words and phrases we use when we think about God and address Him), and of the content, manners, occasions, and places of worship, to describe any deliberate departure from the teaching and example of the Prophet, upon him be peace, in favour of what he is known to have rejected or what he is not known to have authorized. In this narrower, technical sense, *bidʿah* is either an alteration to the religion brought by the Prophet, or it is an addition to it. Religious innovation implies a dissatisfaction with God or His Messenger or with both, since it embodies a judgement that the religion conveyed by, and within the framework, of the Qurʾān and Sunnah is either incorrect or incomplete or both. *Bidʿah* implies a belief that the *dīn*, the Muslim way of life insofar as it is a personal and social effort dedicated to pleasing God, stands in need of improvement. Such need is almost always expressed in the form – 'times have changed', i.e., 'people are not as good as they used to be', or 'you can't halt the march of progress', or 'it is no longer practical to expect people to...'.

The notion that refusal of the Sunnah or indifference to it only happened (or could only ever have happened) in the later periods of Islamic history is based on the wrong kind of idealisation of the first Muslims. In reality, among the early Muslims, there were those who wished to evade one or another *sunnah* for the sake of some private preference, or for what their conscience and experience convinced them was the public good. But they faced strong, authoritative criticism from other Muslims who had a confident grasp of their duty to establish and preserve the *dīn* by conforming their lives to it. What changed in the later periods was that the authoritative critics of departures from the Sunnah were marginalised or silenced. Their voices did not carry enough weight in the public sphere. The good of their personal influence lived on in the circles of their family or close associates but it did not alter general practices or attitudes. Whether for good or bad motives, deviation from the Sunnah was permitted, initially just to cope with historical realities. Over time, such deviations ceased to be viewed as short-term measures. Several factors (notably, relationship between military power and the public authority of religious scholars, and professionalisation or institutionalisation of that authority in the schools and of their texts), operated together to weaken conscientious striving to change realities so that the *sunnah*s could be implemented. Acceptance of deviation opened the way to tolerance of *bidʿah*s until the latter became the established *Islamic* norm. For all practical purposes what had been viewed as *munkar* (rebuked and disapproved) came to be viewed as the *maʿrūf* (the publicly known and approved norm).

It is a duty to resist any such reversal of Islamic norms, and to resist the naming of norms as Islamic that are not so. This effort is required of Muslims regardless of diminution of their power to effect change. It is not different in kind from the effort of those to whom Islam was first presented requiring them to desire and establish the *sunnah*s. We do the first Muslims a disservice if we think this effort was easy, if we think that submitting to God while His Messenger was alive meant that Muslims straightaway acquired a perfected taste for his teachings, a perfected understanding of how these teachings benefited them individually and collectively in their preparation for the Hour. When the ex-polytheists' idols were smashed, they were witnesses that what the idols represented had indeed been worthless: not even the trade of the Makkans and their allies was negatively affected, still less were there disruptions or failures in the processes of nature which they had feared would follow if they ceased to propitiate their inexistent gods. However, the good of the changes demanded in the social order, in relations between men and women, masters and slaves, is not demonstrable in that way. This good requires that it is believed in and striven for, both when the changes in the social order lead to what was hoped for and when they do not. If more harm than good results from a change when it is implemented, or if it leads to neglect of a higher good, then the implementation must be revised, perhaps reversed. But, unless the good envisaged in the change is affirmed when its public implementation is delayed or denied, and unless implementation of the change is permitted and practised somewhere, then that envisaged good is no longer believed in and will pass from the community. All doors to the harms that the change was intended to prevent are then opened. The high cost of refusing a *sunnah* is this: eventually, the opposite of that *sunnah* may become treasured as the *sunnah*.

In my response to the question of how and why the main Sunnī schools of law came to discourage women's attendance at mosque prayers, I try to show in some detail, through the judgments of Abū Ḥanīfah and of others, the tension between knowing and (in their own or others' personal practice) following the *sunnah*, while giving rulings that encourage the opposite. Here, I refer readers to the two Companion ḥadīths (p. vi, facing the very first page of this Preface) about women attending prayers in the mosque.

These reports (recorded in, respectively, the *Ṣaḥīḥ*s of al-Bukhārī and Muslim) concern the family of the caliph, ʿUmar ibn al-Khaṭṭāb. In the first we learn that ʿUmar felt jealous when his wife went out for the *ʿishāʾ* and *fajr* prayers. She was informed of this but continued going to the mosque while ʿUmar refused to forbid her. He refused because the Prophet had forbidden husbands to prevent their wives attending the mosques. In the second, we learn that a grandson of ʿUmar, on hearing of this Prophetic command from his father, ʿAbdullāh ibn ʿUmar, insisted that he and others would, nevertheless, forbid their wives to do the prayers in the mosque. ʿAbdullāh ibn ʿUmar then abused him for this defiance. In the translated text, Ibn Ḥazm cites the famous *ṣaḥīḥ* report of ʿĀʾishah. She said that, had the Prophet seen the 'new thing' that women now are doing, he would not have commended their going to the mosque. But then, as Ibn Ḥazm remarks, she neither stopped herself nor other women going to the mosque.

In the case of ᶜUmar and ᶜĀʾishah, we have, respectively, a private and a public concern that either might have made, but did not make, into a strong enough reason to refuse the *sunnah*. By contrast, as we find in the Ibn Ḥazm text and the background to it (which I tried to make clear in the notes) the rulings attributed to Imāms Mālik and Abū Hanīfah, and consolidated in the schools of the law named after them, do eventually lead to refusal of the *sunnah*. First of all, the status of women going out to attend the prayers in the mosque is changed by these rulings from something *commended* to something *permissible*. Moreover, some restrict that permissibility to older women, presumably because they would not be a temptation *(fitnah)* for the men and therefore for themselves. In time the dominant view came to be that what is *commended*, what is *better*, for women is that they pray at home. Thus, in effect, the *sunnah*-defying preference of ᶜUmar's grandson, which so enraged his father, became prevalent.

For this community, turning away from the Sunnah – not as a temporary measure to deal with some necessity, but as a willed, collective preference that has been allowed to become established – is certain to have grave consequences. But, while we have lived and continue to live with those consequences, we still find it difficult to confront the ways of thinking that opened up a gap between *sunnah* and *fiqh* rulings on this matter. I defer further reflection on that to the Questions and Answers section.

By way of excuses for not bringing this more explicitly to the attention of readers in the first edition, I can only offer the following:

(1) The core of this book is the translated and annotated text from Ibn Ḥazm's *Muḥallā*, where his concern is to correct

the *fiqh* of schools of doctrine that he was in dispute with on points of method and a number of *masāʾil.* The selected text concerns the *masʾalah* of whether it is permissible and commendable for women to go to the mosques to do the daily congregational prayers, even though it is not obligatory for them to do so (there is no dispute that it is obligatory for men). It did not seem to me appropriate to burden his presentation of this issue with what is mentioned but is not central in it. And (2) I already had in mind to write about the *sunnah* vs. *bidʿah* issue with reference to the growing controversy about women-only mosques (i.e., mosques that shut their doors to men) and women imāms (i.e., women leading congregational prayers where women and men are both present), in light of the Muslim feminist critique of *qiwāmah* (roughly, 'patriarchy'), and the carefully nuanced critique of *bidʿah* by Shaykh al-Islam Ibn Taymiyyah.

I am most grateful to those who sent me comments and questions: positive and negative are alike useful in improving my understanding and presentation of the topic. My thanks also, as always, to former colleague and Oxford neighbour Jamil Qureshi, for his help in thinking through and writing up this book.

Mohammad Akram Nadwi
Oxford.
March 2018

Preface to the first edition

Many questions are asked in our time about the rights of women, and about the evident injustices in Islamic societies from arrangements that claim to rest on the authority of the religion. For sure, some of these questions (especially, the manners with which they are asked) derive from perspectives that are aggressively 'modern', that is, hostile to religion generally and to Islam most of all. But it is also true that the same questions can be asked from within self-consciously 'traditional' perspectives, on behalf of the religion, on behalf of its commitment to justice. If that is the case, and it is, we should expect these questions to have been raised from within the boundaries of traditional Islamic scholarship. One such question concerns the right of women to attend the congregational prayers in the mosques, and what right (if any) others have to forbid them.

I had long been aware of Ibn Ḥazm's discussion of this issue in his *Muḥallā*, and its scrupulous, balanced account of the Prophetic and Companion traditions by which it should be resolved. However, it was not until recently, while I was teaching a course on the *Muḥallā* (organized by Cambridge Islamic College, in Queen Mary College, London), that I realized how pressing and important this matter is. It was then that I learnt that, here in the UK, it is not unusual even for Muslim women who are travelling, that is, away from home and in need of a place to do their obligatory prayers, to make their way to a mosque, only to find that they are refused entry. On some occasions, moreover, this refusal was expressed roughly, without sympathy for the need of the women to do their prayers, nor any offer to guide them to some other place where they might pray. In light of such reports, and of the positive response from the students (the men no less than the women) to Ibn Ḥazm's argument on the issue, I felt it would be useful to present it in English for the wider public. In it, the following questions are asked (and, after the weighing of evidence, answered) by Ibn Ḥazm:

> Is it lawful for women to attend congregational prayers in mosques? (Yes.)
>
> Is it lawful for others to forbid this if, for some private or public reason, they happen to dislike it or disapprove of it? (No.)
>
> Is the effort of attending the prayers with the congregation in the mosque more worthy for men than women? (No, it is the same.)
>
> Is it lawful only for elderly women to attend the congregational prayers in the mosques? (No, it is equally lawful for old or young, men or women.)

The notes to the translation of Ibn Ḥazm's text provide references to the ḥadīths that he quotes or mentions, with comments on their status as sound *(ṣaḥīḥ)* or otherwise. Where relevant and useful, the notes also give a brief account of differences of scholarly opinion.

The religious and legal authority of an opinion depends, by consensus of Muslims of all schools, on how securely it is based on the Qurʾān and authenticated Sunnah of God's Messenger, upon him be peace, and how the teachings in these two sources were understood and demonstrated in the practice of the first-comers to Islam, the Companions and their Followers.

God knows best the strength of individual or collective fears, so ingrained in human hearts and habits, which serve as 'necessities' to excuse disobedience to the commands of the religion. So there is a need for flexibility and forbearance with the real-life conditions in particular local neghbourhoods and local situations. But that flexibility should not deter Muslims, men and women alike, from affirming the norms that have the authority of Qurʾān and Sunnah. Even if those norms cannot be implemented, even if they can only be affirmed within a small circle, it is the religious duty of those inside that circle to make others also aware and, to the extent God has willed, strive with good patience and steadfast civility for their wider acceptance.

Mohammad Akram Nadwi
Oxford
January 2015

A wife of ʿUmar ibn al-Khaṭṭāb used to go to the mosque for the prayers of *fajr* and *ʿishāʾ*. It was said to her: Why do you go out when you know that ʿUmar does not like that, and he feels jealous? She said: So what stops him from forbidding me? It was said to her: What stops him is the saying of the Messenger of God, upon him be peace, "Do not stop the women-servants of God from the mosques of God." *(Ṣaḥīḥ al-Bukhārī)*

Sālim ibn ʿAbdullāh ibn ʿUmar informed (us)that ʿAbdullāh ibn ʿUmar said: I heard the Messenger of God, upon him be peace, say: "Do not stop your women from the mosques when they ask your permission to go there." His son Bilāl said to him: By God, we certainly will stop them! Then ʿAbdullāh ibn ʿUmar turned to him, abused him with the most vehement abuse – I never heard him abusing (anyone) like that – and said: I am informing (you of something) from the Messenger of God, upon him be peace, and you say: By God, we certainly will stop them?! *(Ṣaḥīḥ Muslim)*

Introduction

The man, his works and their reputation

ʿAlī ibn Aḥmad ibn Saʿīd ibn Ḥazm (384–456/994–1064),[1] was a leading advocate of the doctrines and method of the Ẓāhirī school, and a great *mujtahid* imām of al-Andalus (Spain). Therefore, the expressions 'al-Ẓahirī' and 'al-Andalūsī' are often added to his name. He was born in Cordoba, where his father was chief vizier at the Umayyad court. The scholarly reputation and social standing of his family must undoubtedly have influenced Ibn Ḥazm in his upbringing and education, and opened doors for him, so that he was soon able to excel in the different sciences of his age.

He studied Arabic language and literature, logic and philosophy, as well as the traditional Islamic disciplines of *ḥadīth* and *fiqh*, under the great masters of the time in Spain. After early completion of his formal education, he too served for a short period in the royal court. However, he soon retired from political office and devoted himself entirely to study, writing and teaching. His vast knowledge of the Islamic sources and

1 These biographical notes on Ibn Ḥazm are based on al-Dhahabī, *Siyar aʿlām al-nubalāʾ*, 18/184–212, *Tadhkirat al-ḥuffāẓ*, 3/1146–55, *Tārīkh al-islām*, parts 451–60; Ibn Khallikān, *Wafayāt al-aʿyān*, 3/325–30; Ibn Ḥajar, *Lisān al-mīzān*, 4/198–202; and Muḥammad Abū Zahrah, *Ibn Ḥazm: fiqhuhū wa-ārāʾuhū*.

a penetrating curiosity and intelligence raised him to the rank of *ijtihād* in *ḥadīth* and *fiqh*.

For a time he adhered to the Shāfiʿī school of law, until his *ijtihād* led him to reject all types of *qiyās* (analogy) and *raʾy* (informed opinion), and to adopt the method of the Ẓāhirīs. He is now acclaimed as the intellectual champion of the Ẓāhirī school, and his writings are treated as the main source of its doctrines, methods and arguments.

According to his son al-Faḍl, Ibn Ḥazm produced some 80,000 pages of writing, consisting of 400 works on *ḥadīth*, *fiqh*, language, logic, philosophy, theology, history and poetry. Among his most important works are: *Kitāb al-Khiṣāl al-ḥāfiẓ li-jumal sharāʾiʿ al-islām* and a commentary on it, *K. al-Īṣl ilā fahm k. al-Khiṣāl*; *al-Mujallā* and the commentary on it, *K. al-Muḥallā fī sharḥ al-Mujallā bi-l-ḥujaj wa-l-āthār*; *K. al-Āthār al-latī ẓāhiruhā al-taʿāruḍ wa-nafy al-tanāquḍ ʿanhā*; *K. al-Jāmiʿ fī ṣaḥīḥ al-ḥadīth*, *K. al-Imlāʾ fī sharḥ al-Muwaṭṭā*; *K. al-Imlāʾ fī qawāʿid al-fiqh*; *K. Durr al-qawāʿid fī fiqh al-ẓāhirīyyah*; *K. al-Iḥkām fī uṣūl al-aḥkām*; and *al-Fiṣal fī al-milal wa-l-niḥal.*

The great Islamic scholars after him paid tribute to him and acknowledged his excellence. Al-Ghazālī (d. 505/1111) said of him: "I found a book on the names of God, Exalted is He, written by Abū Muḥammad ibn Ḥazm al-Andalusī. It is evidence of his great expertise, and the fluency of his mind."[1]

Abū l-Qāsim Ṣāʿid ibn Aḥmad (d. 462/1070) said: "Ibn Ḥazm was, among all the people of al-Andalus, the most comprehensive in the sciences of Islam, the widest among them in knowledge, beside his mastery of linguistics, his full

1 Ibn Ḥajar, *Lisān al-Mīẓān*, 4/201; al-Dhahabī, *Siyar aʿlām al-nubalāʾ*, 18/187.

share in eloquence and poetry, and his knowledge of history and biographies."[1]

Abū ᶜAbdillāh al-Ḥumaydī (d. 488/1095) said: "Ibn Ḥazm was an expert of ḥadīth and *fiqh* of ḥadīth, deriving the rulings from the Book and the Sunnah, having a share in many sciences, and acting upon his knowledge. We have not seen his like in what came together for him of intelligence, sharp memory, generosity of soul and religiosity. He was great of breath and large of hand in literature and poetry. I have not seen anyone compose poetry ex tempore more quickly than him. His poems are abundant."[2]

The Ẓāhirī school is named after Abu Sulaymān Dāwūd ibn ᶜAlī ibn Khalaf al-Ẓāhirī (201–270/816–884)[3]. It is known for its insistence on sticking to the *ẓāhir* or outward sense of expressions in the Qurʾān and ḥadīth texts, and rejection of *qiyās*, *istiḥsān* (preference) and the other methods, sanctioned by most jurists of the other schools, for the derivation of *fiqh*. The Ẓāhirīs do recognize *ijmāᶜ* (consensus) as a source for rulings, but restrict this consensus to the generation of the Companions.

Ibn Ḥazm was very strict in following the principles of his school. He would start his arguments with the Qurʾān, then look to the *ḥadīth*. He accepted only sound Prophetic *ḥadīth*s, and rejected any that had been judged weak or disconnected. He said: "No proof is established by *mawqūf* and *mursal*,[4] nor

---

1 Cited in al-Dhahabī, *Siyar aᶜlām al-nubalāʾ*, 18/187; Ibn Ḥajar, *Lisān al-Mīẓān*, 4/199.

2 al-Dhahabī, *Siyar aᶜlām al-nubalāʾ*, 18/187–8.

3 al-Dhahabī, *Siyar aᶜlām al-nubalāʾ*, 13/97–109.

4 *mawqūf:* a ḥadīth that 'stops' at a Companion, and has not been attributed or traced back to the Prophet himself, upon him be peace; *mursal:* a ḥadīth from a Follower who narrates it as

by anything that is narrated by only those whose religion and memory are not reliable."[1]

Any opinion of a Companion or a Follower or anybody after them is not, by itself, a proof for him. He said: "It is not permissible to leave what has come in the Qurʾān, or has been reported from the Messenger of God, upon him be peace, in a sound narration for the sake of the opinion of a Companion or anyone (else)."[2] "Anyone who abandons the Qurʾān or what has come as sound from the Messenger of God, upon him be peace, for the sake of a Companion or anyone other than him, whether he is the narrator of that report or someone else is, he has surely abandoned what God, Exalted is He, commanded (us) to follow, in favour of the opinion of those, obedience to whom and following whom, God, Exalted is He, never commanded. And (doing) this is opposing the command of God, Exalted is He."[3]

The only *ijmāʿ* that counts for Ibn Ḥazm is the *ijmāʿ* of the Companions. He rejects the idea of adhering to the practice of a city, in the way that some Malikīs claimed to adhere to the practice of Madīnah. He is against any kind of *qiyās*, and he is very harsh in criticizing and refuting all those who adhere to *qiyās*, *rāʾy*, *istiḥsān*, and *maṣlaḥah*. He is very clear that on each and every point of difference, people have no choice but to refer to the Qurʾān and Sunnah. He says: "The obligation is, whenever people differ or anyone disputes an issue, to refer to the Qurʾān and the Sunnah of the Messenger of God, upon him be peace, not to anything else other than them. And it

---

from the Prophet but without identifying the link (i.e., the Companion) between himself and the Prophet.

1 *al-Muḥallā*, 1/51.

2 *al-Muḥallā*, 1/51.

3 *al-Muḥallā*, 1/52.

is not permissible to refer to the practice of the people of Madīnah or other than them."[1]

Besides explaining his own opinions and arguments properly, Ibn Ḥazm is scrupulous in presenting the arguments of others. He quotes (in order of weight of authority) the arguments of the jurists among the Companions and Followers, then those of Abū Ḥanīfah, Mālik, al-Shāfiʿī and others, and discusses and evaluates them in detail. However, his manner when criticizing other scholars could be harsh. Abū l-ʿAbbās ibn al-ʿArīf said: "The tongue of Ibn Ḥazm and the sword of al-Ḥajjāj ibn Yūsuf[2] are twins. This is one of the reasons that the followers of the Ḥanafī and Mālikī *madhhab*s held aloof from him and therefore did not benefit much from him."[3]

This harshness may be partly attributed to his literary talents, including a talent for sarcasm, which he over-indulged at times. It is also attributable in part to his life circumstances: he was persecuted, even imprisoned, for political reasons and for his juristic arguments, his Mālikī enemies being particularly intolerant of him. He felt this intolerance keenly and wished he had been born in the east of the Islamic world, where he thought his work would have been more fairly judged. He wrote: "I am a sun rising in the sky of the sciences, but my fault is that my place of rising is in the West. Had I risen from the East, there

---

1 *al-Muḥallā*, 1/55.

2 al-Ḥajjāj ibn Yūsuf (d. 95/714): the fiercely pro-Umayyad governor of Iraq, noted for draconian efficiency as a military administrator, and depicted as brutally ruthless in the accounts of his contemporaries and in the histories written down subsequently.

3 Abū l-ʿAbbās ibn al-ʿArīf (d. 536/1141), Andalusian Sufi, and the author of *Maḥāsin al-majālis*. His opinion is cited in al-Dhahabī, *Siyar aʿlām al-nubalāʾ*, 18/199.

would have been crowds flocking to pick up what (here) is wasted of my *dhikr* (i.e. my name and fame)."[1]

But Ibn Ḥazm's lapses into sarcasm are not, and should not be, any hindrance to recognizing the honesty and integrity of the evidence he presents and his reasoning with it. Most striking of all is his love for the Prophet, upon him be peace, and his advocacy of strict adherence to the Sunnah. All Muslims can admire him for this love, because it is something that is praised in the Qurʾān, in the Sunnah, and in the sayings of the Companions, as also the sayings of all the imāms of *fiqh* and *ḥadīth* like Abū Ḥanīfah, Mālik, al-Shāfiʿī and Aḥmad ibn Ḥanbal.

Summary of Ibn Ḥazm's arguments on the lawfulness of women attending prayers in the mosques

The text presented and translated here is taken from the *Muḥallā*. This work has been studied and admired, not just in the Ẓāhirī school, but by great scholars associated with the other Sunnī *madhhab*s. Shaykh ʿIzz al-Dīn ibn ʿAbd al-Salām (d. 660/ 1262) said: "I have not seen among the books of Islam anything in the knowledge like *al-Muḥallā* of Ibn Ḥazm, and *K. al-Mughnī* of Shaykh Muwaffaq al-Dīn ibn Qudāmah."[2]

Ibn Ḥazm's argument is that there are well-known ḥadīths that encourage women to attend the prayers in the mosque, and ḥadīths which clearly forbid men to stop women from doing so. Moreover, these ḥadīths are plentiful and sound *(ṣaḥīḥ)* by consensus of the experts in ḥadīth scholarship. They are recorded with several chains of narrations in the

---

1 Cited in al-Dhahabī, *Siyar aʿlām al-nubalāʾ*, 18/208.

2 Cited in al-Dhahabī, *Siyar aʿlām al-nubalāʾ*, 18/193.

two *Ṣaḥīḥ*s (al-Bukhārī and Muslim), as well in the other major compilations. What is found in these texts is further supported by what is known of the practice during the time of the Prophet, upon him be peace, the time of the rightly guided caliphs and the generations after them. Neither the Prophet nor his Companions stopped or discouraged women from going to the mosques to attend congregational prayers.

Ibn Ḥazm also mentions the opinion that it may be permissible for elderly women to go to the mosques, but not for young women. He says there is no evidence for this opinion, having already cited the texts that, to the contrary, establish the right of all Muslims, men and women, young and old alike, to attend the congregational prayers of the Muslims. Interrupting one's routine to go to the mosque entails effort; this effort is recommended for all Muslims alike, and it is rewarding for all Muslims alike. His evidence for this is that the ḥadīths of the Prophet, upon him be peace, on the merits of prayer in congregation do not make a distinction between men and women.

As for those ḥadīths that people refer to when arguing that it is better for women to do their prayers at home, Ibn Ḥazm observes, rightly, that these ḥadīths (with a single possible exception) are all judged to be weak or fabricated: none of them are recorded in the *Ṣaḥīḥ*s of al-Bukhārī and Muslim, nor in the *Muwaṭṭā* of Imām Mālik, nor with a sound chain of narration in any compilation of the ḥadīth. Ibn Ḥazm takes care to present the reasons (also found in the ḥadīth critique of other experts) for considering these ḥadīths to be weak.

Among the sound reports, mentioned by Ibn Ḥazm, that forbid men to stop women attending prayers in the mosque, two are particularly affecting. One concerns ʿUmar ibn al-Khaṭṭāb, the second caliph and perhaps the greatest ruler in

Islamic history. He did not like one of his wives going out to the mosque for the dawn and night prayers because it made him feel jealous. She knew *that* he did not like it, and *why* he did not. Even so, she continued to go, and he never forbade her to go. It was impossible for ʿUmar knowingly to flout an explicit command of the Prophet, upon him be peace. The other report concerns ʿUmar's son ʿAbdullāh, who informed his own sons of that command of the Prophet. One of them, Bilāl, said that husbands (himself included) would, nevertheless, most certainly forbid their wives to go to the mosques. ʿAbdullāh ibn ʿUmar became mightily enraged with him and berated him for rejecting the *sunnah* of the Prophet.

The only sound ḥadīth that has been used to suggest that it is better for women not to go to the mosques but, instead, to pray at home, is reported from ʿĀʾishah. In it she says that, if the Prophet, upon him be peace, had seen the 'new thing' that women have begun doing, he would have stopped them from going to the mosque. Ibn Ḥazm discusses this at length in order to try and understand if its wording can really be taken to mean that women should (now) be stopped from attending the prayers in the mosques. Can a hypothetical condition (if this had happened, then this would have happened) be the basis for a legal judgment, he asks, especially on a matter so central to the everyday life of the believers? He wonders also what this 'new thing' might be that had so upset ʿĀʾishah. He asks why, if misdeeds (such as fornication) that happened during the Prophet's lifetime and for which he ordered punishment, did not lead him to forbid women to come to the mosque, why should this 'new thing' (and we do not know what this is or was) be the basis for changing a ruling of the Prophet, upon him be peace?

Ibn Ḥazm develops other arguments to the effect that this ḥadīth is an expression of ʿĀʾishah's frustration with behaviour that she had observed spreading. (It sounds less like a legal judgement than a remark on the lines of 'If your elders could see you now, they would be so disappointed with you that...'.) Most tellingly, Ibn Ḥazm points out: we may never know what the 'new thing' was, but we do know that ʿĀʾishah never forbade any woman from going to the mosque or anywhere else, nor forbade herself from going to the mosque. It becomes then difficult to understand the *ḥadīth* as forbidding women from attending the prayers in the mosques. Ibn Ḥazm concludes that he prefers to follow the clear practice of ʿĀʾishah.

The importance of following the sunnah on this matter

In certain circumstances, and for their duration, Muslims might advise that women should do the obligatory prayers at home rather than the mosque. This can be a desirable flexibility with norms and rules, to deal with localized necessities that cannot be coped with otherwise. But if the departure from the Prophetic *sunnah* persists and replaces that *sunnah* with some other, then it is certain that the harm that must come to the community from rejecting the instruction of the Prophet, upon him be peace, will indeed befall. A part of that harm is that it becomes very difficult to go back to the original *sunnah*. In some Muslim societies of our day, perhaps in most, the norm is that women do not go to the mosques. Not doing so is what is expected of them by others and by themselves. If women become mindful that they (like the men) should in fact make the effort to go to the mosques, and they do so, it is regarded as 'forward', 'aggressive', even 'impious'. This is individual and collective injustice, and a deeply personal injury to the dignity of believing women. And that is only a part of the harm.

The greater harm is loss of the good from doing the obligatory prayers in congregation in the mosque. It is no fault for women, as it is for men, if they do not go to the mosque, since it is not obligatory on them. Even so, it is equally commended to both and equally rewarded for all who make the effort. When we do *wuḍūʾ* it brings us the good of refreshing and re-orienting our attention, making us ready for the prayer. The effort of leaving our houses or work-places in order to pray in the mosque is a continuation and deepening of that. It is like a miniature *hijrah*, an expressly willed and deliberate shift of perspective. Every stride toward the mosque is rewarded. This little journey can have a profound impact on the quality of intention and attention during the prayer. It declares the public, collective commitment to the institution of *ṣalāh*. It helps to convince us that we are each capable of leaving our private spaces and separate concerns to join in the giving and receiving of mutual encouragement to the good. That strengthens our potential for the realization of other common goods. Being in the mosque enables the people of the locality to exchange goodwill face to face, to learn who is doing well and who may be in want of assistance, and to give and receive knowledge. Women have the same need as men to build and maintain local relationships, and their doing so is a necessary part of the nurture of the young. Had women not attended the Prophet's gatherings in his mosque, we would be deprived of many *ḥadīth*s that have only come to us because women heard them from him and then preserved them.

In sum, praying with others in the mosque multiplies the benefits of prayer many times over, just as the Prophet said. The way back to this *sunnah* is not closed, and *in shāʾa Allāh*, we may recover it through patient education of ourselves and of those willing to listen.

Ibn Ḥazm's argument: Synopsis

Section divisions and the headings for them not found in the original text. These have been supplied by the translator because they provide a useful overview of how Ibn Ḥazm has set out his argument.

Ibn Ḥazm's argument[1]

(Women attending prayers in the mosques)

(318) *Masʾalah* (the issue discussed): If the women attend the prayer along with the men, it is good, because of what has come in the sound *(ṣaḥīḥ)* narration, that they used to attend prayers with the Messenger of God, upon him be peace, and he knew that.[2]

---

1 *al-Muḥallā* (ed. Aḥmad Shākir), 1/126–40. To facilitate comparison with the Arabic text, the numbering of the *masāʾil* (issues discussed) reproduces that in the original; also the page numbers of the original are shown in brackets like this: **(127)**. The subject headings have been added by the translator and are likewise shown in brackets.

2 Ibn Ḥazm mentions some of the very numerous reports on this found in the books of ḥadīth, *sīrah* and Islamic history. A few of these ḥadīths should suffice to establish the fact that women attended the mosque prayers led by the Prophet. For example: Abū Qatādah narrates from the Prophet, upon him be peace, that he said: "I stand in the prayer intending to lengthen it, then I hear the cry of a baby, and I shorten my prayer, because I do not like to make it hard on his mother." Anas narrates, saying: "I have never prayed behind any imām whose prayer is lighter and more complete than the Prophet, upon him be peace. He would hear the cry of a baby, then he would make the prayer lighter, for fear that his mother will be distressed" (al-Bukhārī, *Ṣaḥīḥ*, *Adhān*, b. *man akhaffa al-ṣalāta ʿinda bukāʾ*

(Women praying in a congregation of only women)

(319) *Masʾalah* (the issue discussed): And if women (not in the mosque but with other women) pray in congregation, and one of them leads the prayer, it is still good, because there has not come any text (from the Qurʾān and Sunnah) prohibiting them from that. And the women do not void (*yaqṭaʿu*) each other's prayer,[1] because of the saying of the Messenger of

---

al-ṣabiyy). ʿĀʾishah narrates that once the Messenger of God, upon him be peace, became late for the ʿishā*ʾ* prayer until ʿUmar called him, saying: "The women and children (waiting for the prayer) have fallen asleep..." (al-Bukhārī, *Ṣaḥīḥ*, *Mawāqīt al-ṣalāh*, b. *faḍl al-ʿishāʾ*, b. *al-nawm qabl al-ʿishāʾ li-man ghuliba*; *Adhān*, b. *wuḍūʾ al-ṣibyān...*, b. *khurūj al-nisāʾ ilā al-masājid bi-al-layl wa-al-ghalas*). Sahl ibn Saʿd al-Sāʿidī narrates that the Prophet, upon him be peace, said to the women: "Do not lift your heads (from prostration) until the men are sitting up properly" (al-Bukhārī, *Ṣaḥīḥ*, *Ṣalāh*, b. *idhā kāna al-thawbu ḍayyiqan; al-Adhān, b. ʿaqd al-thiyāb wa-shaddihā...*).

1 According to Ẓāhirī jurists and some jurists of other schools, if a woman passes in front of a man in prayer in such a way that he is distracted, his prayer becomes void. Here, Ibn Ḥazm wants to clarify that this does not apply if a woman passes in front of another woman who is in the prayer. His reasoning is that the women's best row is the last row according to the ḥadīth cited. So when women join the prayer behind the imām they will form their row at the point furthest from the imām; those who come later will make the next row in front of that row, and so on. This implies that women's passing in front of other women in prayer does not void their prayer. (This rule only applies when men and women are praying in the same open space. If the space for women is separated from the space for men by a barrier, the women should make their first row nearest to that barrier, other rows being formed behind them.)

God, upon him be peace: "The best rows of the women are the last ones."[1]

It has been transmitted to us (*ruwwīnā/rawaynā*) from the route (*ṭarīq*) ʿAbd al-Raḥmān ibn Mahdī from Sufyān al-Thawrī from Maysarah ibn Ḥabīb al-Nahdī – he is Abū Khāzim – from Rayṭah al-Ḥanafiyyah, that ʿĀʾishah the mother of the believers led (the women) in the *farḍ* prayer.[2]

And (it has been transmitted to us), from Yaḥyā ibn Saʿīd al-Qaṭṭān from Ziyād ibn Lāḥiq from Tamīmah bint Salamah from ʿĀʾishah the mother of the believers, that she led some women in the *farḍ* of the *maghrib* prayer, and she stood in the middle of them, and she recited the Qurʾān aloud.[3]

---

1 Muslim, *Ṣaḥīḥ*, *Ṣalāh*, b. *taswiyat al-ṣufūf wa-iqāmatihā*; Abū Dāwūd, *Sunan*, *Ṣalāh*, b. *ṣaff al-nisāʾ wa-karāhiyat al-taʾakhkhur ʿan al-ṣaff al-awwal*; al-Tirmidhī, *Jāmiʿ*, *Ṣalāh*, b. *mā jāʾa fī faḍl al-saff al-awwal*; al-Nasaʾī, *Sunan*, *Imāmah*, b. *dhikr khayr ṣufūf al-nisāʾ wa-sharr ṣufūf al-rijāl*; Ibn Mājah, *Sunan*, *Iqāmat al-ṣalāh*, b. *ṣufūf al-nisāʾ*.

2 ʿAbd al-Razzāq, *al-Muṣannaf*, *Ṣalāh*, b. *al-marʾah taʾummu al-nisāʾ*; Ibn Abī Shaybah, *al-Muṣannaf*, *Ṣalāh*, b. *al-marʾah taʾummu al-nisāʾ*; al-Bayhaqī, *al-Sunan al-kubrā*, *Ṣalāh*, b. *al-marʾah taʾummu al-nisāʾ fa-taqūmu wasaṭahunna*.

3 al-Bayhaqī, *al-Sunan al-kubrā*, *Ṣalāh*, *jimāʿ abwāb al-mawāqīt*, b. *karāhiyat taʾkhīr ṣalāt al-ʿaṣr*. There are also many reports from ʿĀʾishah that she used to lead the women in the prayer; these are mentioned in *al-Muṣannaf* of ʿAbd al-Razzāq, *al-Muṣannaf of Ibn Abī Shaybah*, *al-Sunan al-kubrā* of al-Bayhaqī, and other sources.

The editor, Shaykh Muḥammad Aḥmad Shākir was unable to identify Ziyād ibn Lāḥiq and Tamīmah bint Salamah. However, in al-Bayhaqī, *al-Sunan al-kubrā*, both narrators are mentioned with the same names.

(127) And (it has been transmitted to us), from ʿAbd al-Razzāq from Sufyān al-Thawrī[1] from ʿAmmār al-Duhnī from Ḥujayrah bint Ḥuṣayn, that she said: Umm Salamah the mother of the believers led us in the *ʿaṣr* prayer, and she stood in the middle of us.[2]

And (it has been transmitted to us), from Yaḥyā ibn Saʿīd al-Qaṭṭān from Saʿīd ibn Abī ʿArūbah from Qatādah from the mother of al-Ḥasan ibn Abī al-Ḥasan – she is Khayrah, it is her name, she is reliable and well-known – she narrated to them that Umm Salamah the mother of the believers used to lead them (the women) in the prayer during the month of Ramaḍān, and she used to stand with them in their row.[3]

And (it has been transmitted to us), from ʿAbd al-Razzāq from Ibn Jurayj, that he said: Yaḥyā ibn Saʿīd al-Anṣārī informed me (*akhbaranī*) that ʿĀʾishah the mother of the believers used to lead the women in the *nafl* prayer and used to stand in the middle of them.[4]

(128) And (it has been transmitted to us), from ʿAbd al-Razzāq from Ibrāhīm ibn Muḥammad, from Dāwūd ibn al-

---

1 Shākir suggests that the Sufyān here is Sufyān ibn ʿUyaynah, not al-Thawrī. The fact that both Sufyāns narrate from ʿAmmār al-Duhnī may indeed explain a confusion on the part of Ibn Ḥazm that led him to write 'al-Thawrī'. However, when I checked in *al-Muṣannaf*, I found that ʿAbd al-Razzāq writes only 'al-Thawrī', not the rest of the name. So it could be that this ḥadīth is one of several that are narrated by both Sufyāns from the same teachers. Hence, there is no reason to consider, as Shākir does, that Ibn Ḥazm is confused; rather, he has copied the ḥadīth from *al-Muṣannaf* exactly as found there.

2 ʿAbd al-Razzāq, *Muṣannaf*, *Ṣalāh*, b. *al-marʾah taʾummu al-nisāʾ*; Ibn Abī Shaybah, *Muṣannaf*, *Ṣalāh*, b. *al-marʾah taʾummu al-nisāʾ*.

3 Ibn Abī Shaybah, *Muṣannaf*, *Ṣalāh*, b. *al-marʾah taʾummu al-nisāʾ*.

4 ʿAbd al-Razzāq, *Muṣannaf*, *Ṣalāh*, b. *al-marʾah taʾummu al-nisāʾ*.

Ḥuṣayn, from ʿIkrimah, from Ibn ʿAbbās, that he said: 'The woman will lead other women in the *nafl* prayer, while she will stand in the middle of them.'[1]

And it has been narrated from Ibn ʿUmar that he used to command a slave-girl of his to lead his women in the (prayers during the) nights of Ramaḍān.[2]

And from among the Followers *(tābiʿūn)*, it has been transmitted to us from Ibn Jurayj from ʿAṭāʾ,[3] and from the son of Mujāhid from his father,[4] and from Sufyān al-Thawrī from Ibrāhīm al-Nakhaʿi and al-Shaʿbi,[5] and from Wakīʿ from al-Rabīʿ from al-Ḥasan al-Baṣrī, that all of them upheld the permissibility of the woman leading other women in the prayer while standing in the middle of them. ʿAṭāʾ, Mujāhid and al-Ḥasan said: "In the *farḍ* and *nafl*." And others did not forbid that. It is the opinion of Qatādah, al-Awzāʿī, Sufyān al-Thawrī, Isḥāq, Abū Thawr, and the majority of the people of *ḥadīth*. It is also the opinion of Abū Ḥanīfah, al-Shāfiʿī, Aḥmad ibn Ḥanbal, Dāwūd and their companions.[6]

---

1 ʿAbd al-Razzāq, *Muṣannaf*, *Ṣalāh*, b. *al-marʾah taʾummu al-nisāʾ*.

2 Many scholars have cited this report from *al-Muḥallā*; I have not been able to locate it anywhere else.

3 ʿAbd al-Razzāq, *Muṣannaf*, *Ṣalāh*, b. *al-marʾah taʾummu al-nisāʾ*.

4 ʿAbd al-Razzāq, *al-Muṣannaf*, *al-Ṣalāh*, b. *al-marʾah taʾummu al-nisāʾ*.

5 ʿAbd al-Razzāq, *al-Muṣannaf*, *al-Ṣalāh*, b. *al-marʾah taʾummu al-nisāʾ*; Ibn Abī Shaybah, *al-Muṣannaf*, *al-Ṣalāh*, b. *al-marʾah taʾummu al-nisāʾ*.

6 Ibn Qudāmah, the famous Ḥanbalī scholar, says: "Among those from whom it is narrated that the woman can lead other women in the prayer are: ʿĀʾishah, Umm Salamah, ʿAṭāʾ, al-Thawrī, al-Awzāʿī, al-Shāfiʿī, Isḥāq, Abū Thawr. It has been narrated from Aḥmad that it is not recommended. The people of *raʾy* disliked it, and if she has done it (i.e., led the prayer), it will suffice (i.e.,

Sulaymān ibn Yasār and Mālik ibn Anas say: a woman cannot lead other women in a *farḍ* prayer or in a *nafl* prayer.[1] This is an opinion for whose validity there is no evidence. It is also against the opinion of a group of the Companions, and no opponent to (this opinion of theirs) is known from among the Companions, may God be pleased with them. And they (i.e., the followers of Mālik) spread this when it fits in with their following each other *(taqlīd)* (i.e., instead of the *sunnah*).

Moreover, a woman's leading other women in the prayer is included in the saying of God's Messenger, upon him be peace: "Surely, the prayer of the congregation excels the prayer of the individual by twenty-seven times."[2]

---

the prayer will be valid, and they will not need to repeat it). Al-Shaᶜbī, al-Nakhaᶜī and Qatādah say: The woman can lead other women in the *nafl*, but not in *farḍ*" (*al-Mughnī*, 2/468).
The great Ḥanafī jurist, al-Kāsānī says (*Badāʾiᶜ al-ṣanāʾiᶜ*, 1/668): "The woman is suitable for leading the prayer in general, so if she leads other women it will be allowed, and she should stand in the middle of them, because it has been narrated from ᶜĀʾishah, may God be pleased with her, that she led some women in the *ᶜaṣr* prayer and she stood in the middle of them. And (this is) because their state is based on covering, and this (standing within the row) is more covering for her. Yet, their congregation is disliked among us (i.e., Ḥanafīs)." Another Ḥanafī scholar, al-Marghīnānī says (*al-Hidāyah*, 1/236): "It is liked for women to do the congregational prayer alone."

1 Ibn Qudāmah says: "al-Ḥasan and Sulaymān ibn Yasār say: She cannot lead in any *farḍ*, nor in any *nafl*. Mālik says: it is not appropriate for the woman to lead anyone in congregation" (*al-Mughnī*, 2/468).

2 al-Bukhārī, *Ṣaḥīḥ*, *al-Adhān*, b. *faḍl ṣalāt al-jamāᶜah, b. faḍl ṣalāt al-fajr fī jamāᶜah*; Muslim, *Ṣaḥīḥ*, *al-Masājid*, b. *faḍl ṣalāt al-jamāᶜah*. There is no evidence in the Sunnah that women have less reward in this or any other good action, as compared to men.

Then if it is said: So why have you not made (women leading the prayer) a *farḍ* (i.e., obligatory) because of his saying, upon him be peace: "When the time of the prayer comes the eldest of you (m.) should lead in the prayer."[1] We say: had this been (the intended meaning of his instruction) then it would have been allowed for a woman to lead us (i.e., men) in the prayer, and this is impossible. This is an address from him, upon him be peace, (that was) never directed to women who have no man with them. **(129)** (To understand it so) is certainly a mistake in Arabic. And it is impossible and prevented that he, upon him be peace, would commit any mistake in Arabic.

Rather, it was understood generally that the reward of good deeds is not based on gender. For example, the reward of praying in the mosque of the Prophet, upon him be peace, is a thousand times more than in any other mosque other than al-Masjid al-Ḥarām. A woman who was suffering from an illness said: "If God cures me I will set out on journey and I will pray in Bayt al-Maqdis." When she was cured, she prepared for her journey and came to Maymūnah, the wife of the Prophet, upon him be peace, to say *salām* to her, and told her story to her. Upon this, Maymūnah said to her: "Sit down and eat what I have made, and pray in the mosque of the Messenger. I have heard the Messenger of God, upon him be peace, say: 'One prayer in it is better than a thousand prayers in any mosque other than the mosque of the Kaʿbah.' " See Muslim, *Ṣaḥīḥ*, *al-Ḥajj* (without chapter titles); al-Nasaʾī, *Sunan*, *al-Ḥajj*, b. *faḍl al-ṣalāh fī al-masjid al-ḥarām.*

1 The pronoun 'you' is masculine (so too is the verb-form that follows it). Al-Bukhārī, *Ṣaḥīḥ*, *Adhān*, b. *man qāla li-yuʾadhdhin fī al-safar muʾadhdhin wāḥid*, b. *al-adhān li-l-musāfir*, b. *idhā istawaw fī al-qirāʾah fa-lyaʾummahum akbaruhum*; Muslim, *Ṣaḥīḥ*, *Masājid*, b. *man aḥaqqu bi-l-imāmah.*

(Adhān and iqāmah for women)

(320) *Masʾalah*: The *adhān* and *iqāmah* are not (obligatory) on women.[1] But if they say the *adhān* and *iqāmah*, it is good.[2] The argument for that is that the command of God's Messenger, upon him be peace, (to do) the *adhān* is for those on whom the Messenger of God, upon him be peace, has made the prayer in the congregation obligatory by his saying, upon him be peace: "So one of you (m.) should say the *adhān* for you (m.) and the eldest of you (m.) should lead in the prayer."[3] And the women are not commanded (to do) that. So when it is established (that it is not obligatory on the women to say *adhān* and *iqāmah*), the *adhān* is remembrance of God, Exalted is He, and the *iqāmah* is like that. So both of them in their time

1 Among those who say that *adhān* and *iqāmah* are not obligatory on women are: ʿAlī ibn Abī Ṭālib, Ḥasan al-Baṣrī, Muḥammad ibn Sīrīn, ʿAṭāʾ ibn Abī Rabāḥ, Saʿīd ibn al-Musayyab, Ibrāhīm al-Nakhaʿī, al-Zuhrī, Jābir ibn Zayd and al-Ḍaḥḥāk. See Ibn Abī Shaybah, *al-Muṣannaf*, *al-Adhān*, b. *fī al-nisāʾ man qala laysa ʿalayhinna adhānun wa-lā iqāmah*.

2 Sulaymān al-Taymī says: "We asked Anas ibn Mālik: Is there any *adhān* and *iqāmah* (obligatory) upon the women? He answered: No, and if they do so it is a *dhikr* (remembrance) of God." See Ibn Abī Shaybah, *Muṣannaf*, *Adhān*, *fī al-nisāʾ man qāla laysa ʿalayhinna adhānun wa-lā-iqāmah*. Makḥūl says: "If women say *adhān* and *iqāmah*, that is better; and if they do not add to the *iqāmah*, it will suffice them." See al-Bayhaqī, *al-Sunan al-kubrā*, *Ṣalāh*, b. *adhān al-marʾati li-nafsihā wa-ṣawāḥibātihā*.

3 al-Bukhārī, *Ṣaḥīḥ*, *Adhān*, b. *man qāla li-yuʾadhdhin fī al-safar muʾadhdhin wāḥid*, b. *al-adhān li-l-musāfir*, b. *idhā istawaw fī al-qirāʾah fa-lyaʾummahum akbaruhum*; Muslim, *Ṣaḥīḥ*, *Masājid*, b. *man aḥaqqu bi-l-imāmah*.

are good actions.[1] And it has been transmitted to us from Ibn Jurayj from ʿAṭāʾ that he said: "The woman will say the *iqāmah* for herself."[2] Ṭāwūs says: "ʿĀʾishah the mother of the believers used to say the *adhān* and *iqāmah*."[3]

(Unlawfulness of stopping women from going to the mosque)

(321) *Masʾalah*: It is not lawful for the guardian *(walī)* of a woman, or the master of a slave-girl, to stop them attending prayer in congregation in the mosque, if he knows that they intend the prayer. And it is not lawful for (the women) to go out having applied perfume, nor in finery. If she does do (that) then (the guardian) should stop her.

---

1 Ibn Ḥazm means: though not obligatory on them, it is good that women do say the *adhān* and *iqāmah*.

2 ʿAbd al-Razzāq, *al-Muṣannaf, al-Ṣalāh*, b. *hal ʿalā al-marʾati adhānun wa- iqāmah*. Wahb ibn Kaysān says: "Ibn ʿUmar was asked: Is there any *adhān* (obligatory) on the women? He became angry and said: Will I forbid the remembrance of God?" See Ibn Abī Shaybah, *Muṣannaf, Adhān*, b. *man qāla ʿalayhinna an yuʾadhdhinna wa-yuqimna*).

3 ʿAbd al-Razzāq, *Muṣannaf, Ṣalāh*, b. *hal ʿalā al-marʾati adhānun wa- iqāmah?*; Ibn Abī Shaybah, *Muṣannaf, Adhān*, b. *man qāla ʿalayhinna an yuʾadhdhinna wa-yuqimna*. Ibn Abī Shaybah also mentions a few more reports: Hishām says: "Ḥafṣah (bint Sīrīn) used to say *iqāmah* when she prayed." Sālim ibn ʿAbdullāh ibn ʿUmar says: "If women want to, they can say the *adhān*." Jābir ibn ʿAbdullāh says: "A woman can say the *iqāmah* if she wants to."

(Women's prayer in congregation is better than their prayer alone)

And (the women's) prayer in congregation is better than their prayer alone.[1]

(Ḥadīths on not stopping women from going to the mosque)

ᶜAbdullāh ibn Yūsuf has narrated to us (*ḥaddathanā*), saying Aḥmad ibn Fatḥ has narrated to us, saying ᶜAbd al-Wahhāb ibn ᶜĪsā has narrated to us, saying Aḥmad ibn Muḥammad has narrated to us, saying Aḥmad ibn ᶜAlī has narrated to us, saying Muslim ibn al-Ḥajjāj has narrated to us, saying Muḥammad ibn ᶜAbdullāh ibn Numayr has narrated to us, saying my father and ᶜAbdullāh ibn Idrīs narrated to us, both of them saying ᶜUbaydullāh – ibn ᶜUmar (ibn Ḥafṣ ibn ᶜĀṣim ibn ᶜUmar ibn al-Khaṭṭāb) – narrated to us from Nāfiᶜ, from (ᶜAbdullāh) Ibn ᶜUmar, who said: "The Messenger of God, upon him be peace, said: 'Do not stop the women servants of God from the mosques of God.' "[2]

---

1 Ibn Ḥazm's opinion is that the *ḥadīth*s which mention the merit of the prayer in congregation are not specific to men, rather they are general and include both women and men. It is a well-established position of all major jurists that the teachings of the Qurʾān and Sunnah are guidance for all. To exempt women (or men for that matter) from any instruction in those teachings, would need to be based upon clear, sound proofs from the sources.

2 al-Bukhārī, *Ṣaḥīḥ*, *Jumūᶜah* (without chapter headings); Muslim, *Ṣaḥīḥ*, *Ṣalāh*, b. *khurūj al-nisāʾ ilā al-masājid.*

And with the same chain going back to Muslim, who said: Ḥarmalah ibn Yaḥyā narrated to us, saying Ibn Wahb narrated to us saying, Yūnus – ibn Yazīd – informed us from Ibn Shihāb saying Sālim ibn ʿAbdullāh ibn ʿUmar informed (us) that ʿAbdullāh ibn ʿUmar said: "I heard the Messenger of God, upon him be peace, say: 'Do not stop your women from the mosques when they ask your permission to go there.' His (i.e., ʿAbdullāh ibn ʿUmar's) son Bilāl said to him: 'By God, we certainly will stop them!' Then ʿAbdullāh ibn ʿUmar turned to him and abused him with very vehement abuse. I never heard him abusing (anyone) like that, and he said: 'I am informing (you of something) from the Messenger of God, upon him be peace, and you say: By God we will certainly stop them!?' "[1]

And with the same chain going back to Muslim, who said: Abū Kurayb narrated to us, saying Abū Muʿāwiyyah narrated to us, from al-Aʿmash, from Mujāhid, from Ibn ʿUmar, who said: "The Messenger of God, upon him be peace, said: Do not stop the women from going in the night to the mosques."[2]

---

1 Muslim, *Ṣaḥīḥ*, *Ṣalāh*, b. *khurūj al-nisāʾ ilā al-masājid...*; Abū Dāwūd, *Sunan*, *Ṣalāh*, b. *mā jāʾa fī khurūj al-nisāʾ ilā al-masjid.*
In this anger of ʿAbdullāh ibn ʿUmar there is a great lesson for all those who stop women from going to the mosque. It is on the account of this ḥadīth of the Prophet, upon him be peace, that ʿAbdullāh's father, ʿUmar ibn al-Khaṭṭāb did not dare to forbid his wife ʿĀtikah from going to the mosque. This is discussed further below.
Even those early jurists who disliked women going to the mosque did not stop them from doing so. Rather, all the compilations of *fiqh* discuss in great detail the order of the rows of men and women in the congregational prayers in the mosques.

2 al-Bukhārī, *Ṣaḥīḥ*, *Jumūʿah* (no chapter heading); Muslim, *Ṣaḥīḥ*, *Ṣalāh*, b. *khurūj al-nisāʾ ilā al-masājid...*; al-Bukhārī (in

Ḥamām narrated to us, saying ʿAbbās ibn Aṣbagh narrated to us, saying Muḥammad ibn ʿAbd al-Malik ibn Ayman narrated to us, saying Muḥammad ibn Waḍḍāḥ narrated to us, saying: Ḥāmid – ibn Yaḥyā – al-Balkhī narrated to us, saying Sufyān – ibn ʿUyaynah – narrated to us from Muḥammad ibn ʿUmar ibn ʿAlqamah ibn Waqqāṣ, from Abū Salamah ibn ʿAbd al-Raḥmān ibn ʿAwf, from Abū Hurayrah, who said: the Messenger of God said: "Do not stop the women slaves of God from the mosques of God, while they do not go out except as *tafilāt*."[1]

ʿAlī (Ibn Ḥazm) says: And *al-tafilah* is the woman without perfume and without attractive clothing.

ʿAbdullāh ibn Yūsuf narrated to us, saying Aḥmad ibn Fatḥ narrated to us, saying ʿAbd al-Wahhāb ibn ʿĪsā narrated to us, saying Aḥmad ibn Muḥammad narrated to us, saying Aḥmad ibn ʿAlī narrated to us, saying Muslim ibn al-Ḥajjāj narrated to us, saying Abū Bakr ibn Abī Shaybah narrated to us, saying Yaḥyā ibn Saʿīd al-Qaṭṭān narrated to us from Muḥammad ibn ʿAjlān, who said: Bukayr ibn ʿAbdillāh ibn al-Ashajj narrated to us from Busr ibn Saʿīd, from Zaynab the wife of ʿAbdullāh ibn Masʿūd, who said, the Messenger of

---

Ṣaḥīḥ, *Adhān*, b. *khurūj al-nisāʾ ilā al-masājid bi-l-layl wa-l-ghalas*; b. *istiʾdhān al-marʾati zawjaha bi-l-khurūji ilā al-masjid*; *Nikāḥ*, b. *istiʾdhān al-marʾati zawjahā fī al-khurūj ilā al-masjidi wa-ghayrihī*) has also narrated this ḥadīth through the chain of Sālim from Ibn ʿUmar from the Prophet, upon him be peace, who said: "When your women ask your permission to go the mosques at night then give them permission."

1 Abū Dāwūd, Sunan, *Ṣalāh*, b. *mā jāʾa fī khurūj al-nisāʾ ilā al-masjid.*

God, upon him be peace, said to us (women): "When one of you attends the mosque, she should not put on any perfume."[1]

And from the route of Mālik, from Yaḥyā ibn Saʿīd, from ʿAmrah bint ʿAbd al-Raḥmān, from ʿĀʾishah the mother of the believers, who said: Indeed the Messenger of God, upon him be peace, used to pray the morning prayer, then **(131)** the women used to turn (from the mosque) covered in their cloaks, not being recognized because of the darkness.[2]

Aḥmad ibn Muḥammad ibn al-Jasūr narrated to us, saying Muḥammad ibn ʿAbdillāh ibn Abī Dulaym narrated to us, saying Ibn Waḍḍāḥ narrated to us, saying Abū Bakr ibn Abī Shaybah narrated to us, saying Ḥusayn ibn ʿAlī – al-Juʿfī – narrated to us from Zāʾidah, from Abdullāh ibn Muḥammad ibn ʿAqīl, from Jābir, from the Messenger of God, upon him be peace, who said: "The best of the rows for the men is the front one, and the worst of the rows of the men is the back one, and the worst of rows for the women is the front one, and the best of rows for the women is the back one. O party of the women! when the men prostrate, then lower your gaze, so your eyes do not fall upon the private parts of the men because of the tightness of their lower garments."[3]

ʿAbdullāh ibn Rabīʿ narrated to us, saying: Muḥammad ibn Isḥāq narrated to us, saying: Ibn al-Aʿrābī narrated to me, saying:

---

1 Muslim, *Ṣaḥīḥ*, *Ṣalāh*, b. *khurūj al-nisāʾ ilā al-masājid...*

2 al-Bukhārī, *Ṣaḥīḥ*, *Ṣalāh*, b. *fī kam tuṣallī al-marʾatu min al-thiyāb*; *Mawāqīt al-ṣalāh*, b. *waqt al-fajr*; *Adhān*, b. *intiẓār al-nas qiyam al-imām al-ʿālim*, b. *surʿat insiraf al-nisāʾ min al-subh wa-qillati muqamihinna fī al-masjid*; Muslim, *Ṣaḥīḥ*, *Masājid*, b. *istiḥbāb al-tabkīr bi-l-ṣubḥ fī awwali waqtihā.*

3 Ibn Abī Shaybah, *Muṣannaf*, *Ṣalāh*, b. *man kariha li-l-nisāʾ idhā ṣallayna maʿa al-rijāl an yarfaʿna ruʾūsahunna qablahum*; Aḥmad ibn Ḥanbal, *al-Musnad*, *musnad Jābir.*

Abū Dāwūd narrated to us, saying: ʿAbdullāh ibn ʿAmr – Abū Maʿmar – narrated to us, saying: ʿAbd al-Wārith ibn Saʿīd – al-Tannūrī – narrated to us, saying: Ayyūb – al-Sakhtiyānī – narrated to us from Nāfiʿ, from Ibn ʿUmar, who said, the Messenger of God, upon him be peace, said: "What if we leave this door (of the mosque) for the women?" Then Ibn ʿUmar never entered from that door until he died.[1]

And with the same (chain of narration going back) to Abū Dāwūd, who said: Qutaybah narrated to us, saying Bakr ibn Muḍar narrated to us from ʿAmr ibn al-Ḥārith, from Bukayr - ibn al-Ashajj - from Nāfiʿ, who said: "ʿUmar ibn al-Khaṭṭāb used to forbid (men) **(132)** from entering from *bāb al-nisāʾ* (the door of the women in the mosque of the Prophet).[2]

ʿAlī (i.e., Ibn Ḥazm) says: Had the prayer of the women in their homes been better, then the Messenger of God, upon him be peace, would not have let them (the women) undergo a hardship which does not bring to them any extra merit, or which rather lowers their merit. And this would not be sincere advice, whereas he, upon him be peace, says: "The religion is sincere advice (*naṣīḥah*)."[3] He, upon him be peace, is far away from that (i.e., giving insincere advice). Rather, he is the most sincere of all the creatures to his *ummah*. Had that been the case (i.e., the prayer of the women at home being better), then he, upon him be peace, would not have made it obligatory not to stop women (from going to the mosque), and he would not have commanded women to go out as *tafilāt* (without perfume and attractive clothing).

1 Abū Dāwūd, *Sunan*, *Ṣalāh*, b. *al-tashdīd fī dhālik*.

2 Abū Dāwūd, *Sunan*, *Ṣalāh*, b. *iʿtizāl al-nisāʾ fī al-masājid ʿan al-rijāl*.

3 Muslim, *Ṣaḥīḥ*, *Īmān*, b. *bayān anna al-dīn al-naṣīḥah*.

The least (that can be taken) from this is that it is a command of recommendation and encouragement.

(Those who prefer that women pray at home)

Abū Ḥanīfah and Mālik say: "(The women's) prayer in their homes is better." And Abū Ḥanīfah disliked their going out to the mosques for the prayer of the congregation, for the Friday prayer, and on the two *ʿīd*s.[1] He made concession for the elderly woman, specifically in the late night prayer and the morning prayer, and it has also been narrated from him that he did not dislike their going out on the *ʿīd*s.

Mālik said: "We do not stop (the women) from going out to the mosques." And he allowed the aged elderly woman to attend the two *ʿīds* and the *istisqāʾ* (prayer for rain).[2] He said: "The young woman may go out to the mosque occasionally." He said: "The aged elderly woman may go to the mosque, but should not go too often."[3]

---

1 Muḥammad al-Shaybānī says (*al-Ḥujjah ʿalā ahl al-madīnah*, 1/200–1): "Abū Ḥanīfah says about women going out on the two *ʿīd*s: it was allowed in the past. As for now, it is not appropriate except for an aged old lady; then there is no harm in her going out."

2 Muḥammad al-Shaybānī says (*al-Ḥujjah ʿalā ahl al-madīnah*, 1/201): "The people of Madīnah say about women going out on the two *ʿīd*s: it has not come to our knowledge that it is obligatory upon them."

3 According to Aḥmad ibn Ḥanbal, it is allowed for women to go out for the *ʿīd* prayer, but it is not recommended. Ibn Qudāmah says (*al-Mughnī*, 3/119–20): "There is no harm in women's going out on the day of *ʿīd* to the place of *ʿīd* prayer. Ibn Ḥāmid says: that is recommended."

(Arguments of those who dislike women attending prayers in the mosques)

ᶜAlī (Ibn Ḥazm) says: those who disliked (women's going to the mosque) raised noisy protest (against me) using a narration that has been transmitted to us from Sufyān, from Yaḥyā ibn Saᶜīd, from ᶜAmrah, from ᶜĀᵓishah, who said: "Had the Messenger of God, upon him be peace, seen what the women have invented after him, he would have stopped them from the mosque as the women of the children of Israel have been stopped."[1]

And (they argued the same opinion) from another ḥadīth, which has been narrated from ᶜAbd al-Ḥamīd ibn al-Mundhir al-Anṣārī, from his paternal aunt or his grandmother **(133)** Umm Ḥumayd, that the Prophet, upon him be peace, said: "Your prayer in your house is better than your prayer with me."[2]

(134)) And (they argued the same opinion) from another ḥadīth, which has been narrated from the route of ᶜAbdullāh ibn Rajāᵓ al-Ghudānī who said: Jarīr ibn Ḥāzim[3] informed us from Abū Zurᶜah ibn ᶜAmr ibn Jarīr that Abū Hurayrah narrated to him that the Prophet, upon him be peace, said:

---

1 al-Bukhārī, *Ṣaḥīḥ*, *Adhān*, b. *intiẓār al-nās qiyām al-imām al-ᶜālim*; Muslim, *Ṣaḥīḥ*, *Ṣalāh*, b. *khurūj al-nisāᵓ ilā al-masājid.*

2 Ibn Abī Shaybah, *Muṣannaf*, *Ṣalāh*, b. *man kariha dhālik*; Aḥmad ibn Ḥanbal, *al-Musnad*, *musnad al-nisāᵓ*.

3 Ibn Ḥazm has erred here. The narrator's name is Jarīr ibn Ayyūb al-Bajalī, not Jarīr ibn Ḥāzim. This will be discussed later with the discussion of Ibn Ḥazm's explanation of the weakness of this narration.

"The woman's prayer in her secluded room is greater for her reward than her prayer in her house, and her prayer in her house is greater for her reward than her prayer in her *dār*, and that her prayer in her *dār* is greater for her reward than her prayer in the mosque of her people, and her prayer in the mosque of her people has greater reward than praying in the mosque of congregation, and her prayer in the mosque of congregation is better than going out to the prayer on the day of *ʿīd*."

(Their misinterpretation of the ḥadīth in which the Prophet encourages women to go out for the ʿīd prayer)

Some of them have said: Perhaps the Messenger of God, upon him be peace, commanded their going out on the day of *ʿīd*[1] to awe the enemy because of the small number of Muslims at that time, so they would appear numerous in the sight of those who saw them.

ʿAlī (ibn Ḥazm) says: this is a great (sin), because it is a lie against the Messenger of God, upon him be peace, and it is

1 This refers to the famous sound ḥadīth of Umm ʿAṭiyyah al-Anṣāriyyah: "We were commanded to bring out, on the days of the two *ʿīd*s, the menstruating women and the protected young girls, so they might attend the congregation of Muslims and their supplication. And the menstruating women were to keep apart from the place of the prayer. A woman said: O God's Messenger, if one of us has no *jilbāb*? He answered that another woman should give her her *jilbāb*." See al-Bukhārī, *Ṣaḥīḥ*, *Ḥayḍ*, b. *shuhūd al-ḥāʾiḍ al-ʿīdayn...*; *Ṣalāh*, b. *wujūb al-ṣalāh fī al-thiyāb*; *ʿĪdayn*, b. *al-takbīr ayyāma minan wa-idhā ghadā ilā ʿarafah*, b. *khurūj al-nisāʾ wa-l-ḥuyyaḍ ilā al-muṣallā*, b. *idhā lam yakun lahā jilbāb fī al-ʿīd*, b. *iʿtizāl al-ḥuyyaḍ al-muṣallā*; *Ḥajj*, b. *taqḍī al-ḥāʾiḍu al-manāsika kullahā*; Muslim, *Ṣaḥīḥ*, *Ṣalāt al-ʿīdayn*, b. *dhikr ibāḥat khurūj al-nisāʾ fī al-ʿīdayn*.

an utterance without knowledge. And he, upon him be peace, has explained that his command of (the women's) going out is so that they should attend the good and the supplication of Muslims, while the menstruating women avoided the place of prayer. So reproach to the one who belies the word of the Prophet, upon him be peace, and invents a lie by his own opinion. Moreover, this opinion, beside being a sheer lie, is cold and very silly. Because the Prophet, upon him be peace, was not in the presence of an army, so he would have to awe them. There was no enemy with him except the hypocrites and Jews of Madīnah, those who knew that they are women. So be amazed by this mess (of an explanation)![1]

---

1 This explanation is indeed shocking, that the Prophet, upon him be peace, only commanded women to go out for the *ᶜīd* prayer to make show of the Muslims' numbers and so awe the enemy. Had this been the case, women would have stopped doing so when the Muslim population grew. In fact, this *sunnah* continued from the time of the Prophet, upon him be peace, through the time of the Companions, the Followers and the generations after them, when the Muslims held great political and military power in the world, and had no need to awe their enemies by showing their number. Here are a few more narrations: 1) Ibn ᶜAbbās narrates that the Messenger of God, upon him be peace, used to take his daughters and his wives out to both *ᶜīd*s. 2) ᶜĀʾishah says: The virgin girls used to come out because of the command of the Messenger to go out for the two *ᶜīd*s. 3) Abū Bakr al-Ṣiddīq said: It is obligatory upon every woman to go out to both *ᶜīd*s. 4) ᶜAlī said: It is obligatory upon every woman to go out to both *ᶜīd*s. 5) ᶜAbdullāh ibn ᶜUmar used to take out those of his family who could do so, to attend both *ᶜīd*s. 6) ᶜAlqamah and Aswad used to take their women out on both *ᶜīd*s. 7) Abū Isḥāq al-Sabīᶜī said: Abū Maysarah's wife used to go out for the *ᶜid*. See Ibn Abī Shaybah, *Muṣannaf*, *Ṣalāh*, *man rakhkhaṣa fī khurūj al-nisāʾ ilā al-ᶜidayn*.

(Interpretations of the ḥadīth of ʿĀʾishah)

ʿAlī (Ibn Ḥazm) says: As for the ḥadīth of ʿĀʾishah, there is no proof in it for a number of reasons:

The first one is that he, upon him be peace, did not see this 'new thing' that women had invented, so he did not stop them. Since he did not stop them, then your stopping them is a *bidʿah* and an error. And this is like His saying, Exalted is He: "O wives of the Prophet, whoever of you were to commit **(135)** a clear immorality, for her the punishment would be twice doubled."[1] But they never committed any immorality, and the punishment was not twice doubled for them, and all praise is due to God the Lord of the worlds. This is also like His saying, Exalted is He: "And if only the people of the cities had believed and feared God, We would have opened upon them blessings from the heaven and the earth."[2] But they did not believe, so the blessings were not opened upon them.

And we do not know of a sillier argument than the argument of the one who argues by someone saying – had such and such been, then such and such would have been – to make obligatory what has not been, the thing that, had it been, then that other also would have been.

The second reason is that God, Exalted is He, knew what women would invent. Anyone who denies this would have committed unbelief. But He never revealed to His Prophet, upon him be peace, to stop the women (from going to the mosque) because of what they would have sought to invent. Nor did He, Exalted is He, reveal to him: Tell the people: when the women invent new things, then stop them from

1 Qurʾān, *al-Aḥzāb*, 33:30.
2 Qurʾān, *al-Aʿrāf*, 7:96.

the mosques. Since God, Exalted is He, did not do this, then relying upon such a saying is silly and an error.

The third reason is that we do not know what the 'new thing' was that the women did that they had not done at the time of the Messenger of God, upon him be peace. Whatever it is, it could not be worse than fornication. And the fornication itself happened in the time of the Messenger of God, upon him be peace, and he stoned in it and flogged, and he never stopped the women (from going to the mosque) because of that. Moreover, fornication is just as unlawful for men as it is for women, and there is no difference. So what has made fornication a cause to stop the women from the mosques, and has not made it a cause to stop the men from the mosques? This is a reasoning that God, Exalted He is, never has been pleased with, nor His Messenger, upon him be peace.

The fourth reason is that the 'new thing' that was happening, was done, undoubtedly, by some women only, not others. Thus it is impossible to stop a general good from those who did not do this 'new thing', because of those people who did that 'new thing', except if a text comes from God, Exalted is He, on the tongue of His Messenger, upon him be peace, then he would be listened to and obeyed.[1] God, Exalted is He, has said: 'And no soul earns (reproach) except against itself, and no bearer of burdens will bear the burden of another.'[2]

---

1 Ibn Qudāmah says: "ʿĀʾishah's saying is specific to those women who did the new things, not others, and no doubt it will be disliked for those women. Rather, it is recommended for the women to go out without applying any perfume and not wearing any clothes or displaying an adornment" (*al-Mughnī*, 3/120).

2 Qurʾān, *al-Anʿām*, 6:164.

The fifth reason is that if this 'new thing' is a reason to stop women **(136)** from going to the mosque, then more preferably, it should undoubtedly be a cause to stop them from going to the market and from any public way! Then why have these people specified stopping them from the mosque because of the 'new thing' that they did, while not stopping them from the other ways? Moreover, Abū Ḥanīfah allowed a woman to be travelling alone and walking in the desert and forest for the distance of two and half days (travelling), and he did not dislike it for her.[1] That is how messing up (an argumentation) should go!

The sixth reason is that ʿĀʾishah herself did not, because of that, hold the opinion of stopping the women (from going to the mosque), nor did she say (to the men): stop the women because of the 'new thing' that they have done. Rather, she just informed that if he, upon him be peace, had been alive, he would have stopped them. This is exactly our opinion. We say: if he, upon him be peace, had stopped them we would have stopped them. So since he did not stop them, we will not stop them. They (those who dislike women going to the mosques) have not achieved (anything) except opposing the *sunnah*, and opposing ʿĀʾishah, may God be pleased with her, and lying by suggesting to their imitators in ambiguity that by that ḥadīth of hers she forbade the going out of the women. Rather, she did not do that.[2] We seek refuge in God from withholding His help from us.

---

1 Ibn Ḥazm is scoring a sarcastic point here at the expense of those who allow women to travel alone without being accompanied by their husbands or any *maḥram* for a distance of less than three days' travelling, but do not allow them to walk the short distance to the mosques in their neighbourhoods.

2 I.e., ʿĀʾishah continued going to the mosque for the prayers

(Weakness of the ḥadīths preferring women to pray at home)

As for the *ḥadīth* of ʿAbd al-Ḥamīd ibn al-Mundhir: he is *majhūl*, it is not known who he is.[1] It is not permissible to abandon the *mutawātir*[2] narrations of the reliable people because of the narration of one of whom it is not known who he is.[3]

As for the *ḥadīth* of ʿAbdullāh ibn Rajāʾ al-Ghudānī: he is a man of abundance of alteration (*taṣḥīf*) and mistake (*ghalaṭ*), and he is not a proof. That is what ʿAmr ibn ʿAlī al-Fallās and others have said about him.[4]

---

herself, and she never stopped any woman from doing so.

1 This ḥadīth has been narrated by two routes: 1) the route of ʿAbd al-Ḥamīd ibn al-Mundhir, which Ibn Ḥazm has cited, and which is recorded by Ibn Abī Shaybah in his *Muṣannaf*, and 2) the route of ʿAbdullāh ibn Suwayd al-Anṣārī, which Aḥmad ibn Ḥanbal has recorded in his *Musnad*. Both these routes are weak. As for ʿAbd al-Ḥamīd ibn al-Mundhir: he is not known, as Ibn Ḥazm says. In some books his name has been mentioned as Saʿīd ibn al-Mundhir, also an unknown person. And, similarly, ʿAbdullāh ibn Suwayd al-Anṣārī is unknown. Some people have confused this ʿAbdullāh with ʿAbdullāh ibn Suwayd, who was a Companion.

2 *mutawātir:* a narration that is widely current, having been narrated by many from many. This usually means that the ḥadīth is remembered from a public occasion when many heard the same Prophetic discourse.

3 Ibn Khuzaymah also doubted the soundness of those ḥadīths that prefer women's prayer at home. See his *Ṣaḥīḥ*, *Ṣalāh*, *jimāʿ abwāb ṣalāt al-nisāʾ fī al-jamāʿah*, b. *ikhtiyār ṣalāt al-marʾah fī baytihā ʿala ṣalātihā fī al-masjid.*

4 See the entry for ʿAbdullāh ibn Rajāʾ al-Ghudānī in al-Mizzī, *Tahdhīb al- kamāl*, vol. 14. In this ḥadīth, ʿAbdullāh b. Rajāʾ is

Now if this report and the report of ʿAbdullāh ibn Rajāʾ al-Ghudānī had been sound – but they are not sound – then in their details there would have been a contradiction of the firmly established reports that we have already mentioned, and of his command, upon him be peace, that (the women) should go out, even the protected virgin girls and the menstruating women, to attend the prayer of *ʿīd.* He even commanded the woman who has no *jilbāb* to borrow a *jilbāb* from other women for that purpose.[1]

It (would also have been contradicting) what ʿAbdullāh ibn Rabīʿ has narrated to us, saying Muḥammad ibn Isḥāq narrated to us, saying Ibn al-Aʿrābī narrated to us, saying Abū Dāwūd narrated to us, saying: Muḥammad ibn al-Muthannā narrated to us that ʿAmr ibn al-ʿĀṣim al-Kilābī narrated to them, who said: Hammām – he is ibn Yaḥyā – narrated to us from Qatādah, from Muwarriq al-ʿIjlī from Abū al-Aḥwaṣ, from ʿAbdullāh **(137)** ibn Masʿūd, from the Prophet, upon him be peace, who said: "The prayer of the woman in her house is better than her prayer in her room, and her prayer in her mosque *(fī masjidihā)*[2] is better

---

not the main problem. Rather, the problem is Jarīr ibn Ayyūb al-Bajalī. Ibn Ḥazm misread him as Jarīr ibn Ḥāzim who is a reliable narrator and expert of ḥadīth. Jarīr ibn Ayyūb al-Bajalī has been accused by the experts as a fabricator, and discredited strongly by people like al-Bukhārī, Abū Ḥātim al-Rāzī, al-Nasaʾī and others. See Ibn Ḥajar, *Lisān al-mīzān*, entry for Ayyūb.

1 In the famous ḥadīth, already mentioned, of Umm ʿAṭiyyah, recorded in the two *Ṣaḥīḥ*s and other collections.

2 Perhaps the wording *fī masjidihā* is what Ibn Ḥazm read in his copy of Sunan of Abū Dāwūd, which follows the narration of Ibn al-Aʿrābī. However, in the narration of Abū ʿAlī al-Luʾluʾī, which has been popular in the eastern Islamic world, the wording is *fī makhdaʿihā*, meaning in her small room (within the house). This explanation is no more than a possibility; what

than her prayer in her house."[1]

ʿAlī (Ibn Ḥazm) says: He intends, no doubt, the mosque of her quarter. Because if he, upon him be peace, had intended the mosque of her house, then he would have been saying: her prayer in her house is better than her prayer in her house. He, upon him be peace, is far from saying the impossible.[2]

That being so, it is right to say that one of the two commands is abrogated. Either his saying her prayer in her mosque is better than her prayer in her home, and his encouraging, upon him be peace, the (women's) going out to the *ʿīd* and to the mosque, are abrogated by his saying that her prayer in her house is better than her prayer in the mosque, and better than her going out to the *ʿīd* prayer. Or his saying, upon him be peace, that her prayer in her home is better than her prayer in her mosque, and her prayer in her mosque is better than her going out to the *ʿīd* prayer, are abrogated by his saying, upon him be peace that her prayer in her mosque is better than her prayer in her house, and (abrogated) by his encouragement of the woman to go out to the *ʿīd* prayer.

There is no escape from one of these two matters. And it is not permissible to affirm the abrogation of any sound report except by a proof (equally sound or more sound).

---

is more likely is that Ibn Ḥazm simply misread this word.

1 Abū Dāwūd, *Sunan*, *Ṣalāh*, b. *al-tashdīd fī dhālika*.

2 This comment is based on Ibn Ḥazm's misreading of the wording of the ḥadīth. In any case, this ḥadīth of Abū Dāwūd is a weak one. Ibn Khuzaymah (*Ṣaḥīḥ*, *Ṣalāh, jimāʿ abwāb ṣalāt al-nisāʾ fī al-jamāʿah*, b. *ikhtiyār ṣalāt al-marʾah fī baytihā ʿalā ṣalātihā fī al-masjid*) says there is doubt as to Qatādah hearing this ḥadīth from Muwarriq al-ʿIjlī. According to al-Dāraquṭnī (*al-ʿIlal*, 5/314), there is an inconsistency in the *isnād* of the ḥadīth and divergence among its narrators about its being *marfūʿ* (a Prophetic) or *mawqūf* (a Companion ḥadīth).

So we looked into that and we found that the (women's) going out to the mosque and the place of the *ʿīd* prayer is an act additional to **(138)** the prayer, and a trouble – in the dawns, darkness, crowds, hot noons, rains and cold. So had the merit of this additional act been abrogated, then necessarily, (their going to the mosque) will not be void of two ways, and there is no third to them: either her praying in the mosque and the place of *ʿīd* prayer will be equal to her praying in her home, then all this action would have been useless and void, an unnecessary going to trouble and hardship. And it cannot at all be otherwise, but (the opponents of our position) do not say this. Or her praying in the mosques and the place of the *(ʿīd)* prayer will have less reward, as compared to her praying in her home, as the opponents do say. Then, in this case, all the above-mentioned action would be sinful and decreasing the merit (of the prayer). For, no additional act decreases the merit of any prayer compared to the same prayer (without that addition) except if it is forbidden, and other than this is not possible. This does not come under the heading of leaving recommended actions in the prayer – that does decrease the reward if one does (it) – because (the one who does) this has not committed any sin, rather he has abandoned acts of merit. As for the one who made effort to do something in the prayer, then he lost some of his reward which he would have obtained had he not done it, and destroyed some of his action, then this is a forbidden act without any doubt. Other than this is not possible. In the act which is disliked there is never a sin nor destruction of any (good) action, rather it has (in it) no reward and no sin at the same time. The sin and the destruction of the (good) action is only in committing the forbidden act.

(The Prophet and the rightly guided caliphs never stopped women from going to the mosques)

All the people of the earth agree that the Messenger of God, upon him be peace, never stopped the women from praying with him in his mosque until he died, nor did the rightly guided caliphs do this after him.[1] (Only) then would

1 There are many reports affirming the continuity of this *sunnah* among Muslims from the time of the Prophet. For example: Umm Salamah narrates that when the Messenger of God, upon him be peace, would say the *salām* (at the end of the prayer) the women would stand up when he finished (saying) the *salām*, and he would remain in his place for a while before getting up. Al-Zuhrī, one of the narrators of this ḥadīth, says: 'We think – God knows best – that was to let the women go back from the mosque, before the men could catch (sight of) them' (al-Bukhārī, *Ṣaḥīḥ*, *Adhān*, b. *ṣalāt al-nisāʾ khalf al-rijāl*; b. *mukth al-imām fī muṣallāhu baʿd al-salām*). Umm al-Faḍl narrates that the last thing that she heard from the Prophet, upon him be peace, was *Sūrat al-Mursalāt*, which he read in the prayer of *maghrib* (al-Bukhārī, *Ṣaḥīḥ*, *Adhān*, b. *al-qirāʾah fī al-maghrib*). ʿĀʾishah narrates that the wives of the Prophet, upon him be peace did *iʿtikāf* after his death (al-Bukhārī, *Ṣaḥīḥ*, *Abwāb al-iʿtikāf*, b. *al-iʿtkāf fī al-ʿashr al-awākhir*; Muslim, *Ṣaḥīḥ*, *Iʿtikāf*, b. *iʿtikāf al-ʿashr al-awākhir*); Ibrāhīm al-Nakhaʿī, who is a younger *tābiʿī*, says: "The wife of Abū Masʿūd al-Anṣārī used to pray the late night prayer in the congregational mosque" (Ibn Abī Shaybah, *Muṣannaf*, *Ṣalāh*, b. *man rakhkhaṣa li al-nisāʾ fī al-khurūj ilā al-masjid*). ʿAbd al-Malik ibn Marwān, the great Umayyad caliph, used to sit in the assembly of Umm al-Dardāʾ in the back of the great mosque in Damascus, and at the time of the prayer he would lead the prayer, and help her to join the women's rows (al-Dhahabī, *Siyar aʿlām al-nubalāʾ*, 4/279).
In the course of research on the women scholars of *ḥadīth*,

it have been correct to say that it is an abrogated act. Since there is no doubt in this, then it is an act of virtue. Had that not been the case, then he, upon him be peace, would not have approved it and would not have let women make effort for this trouble without any benefit, rather with a harm. And this is hardship (*al-ʿusr*) and hurt (*al-adhā*), not sincerity.[1] Since there is no doubt in this, then it is abrogating and the other one is abrogated.

This is (the case) if both those ḥadīths had been sound. So how then when they are not sound?

It has been transmitted to us from the route of ʿAbd al-Razzāq from Sufyān al-Thawrī, from Hishām ibn ʿUrwah, who said **(139)** that ʿUmar ibn al-Khaṭṭāb commanded Sulaymān ibn Abī Ḥathmah to lead the women at the back of the mosque in the month of Ramaḍān.[2]

And (it has been transmitted to us) from ʿAbd al-Razzāq, from Maʿmar, from al-Zuhrī that ʿĀtikah bint Zayd ibn ʿAmr ibn Nufayl was married to ʿUmar ibn al-Khaṭṭāb. She used to

---

I found many hundreds of examples of women studying or teaching in all major mosques of the Ḥijāz, Syria, Iraq, Egypt and other parts of the Muslim world. (For details, see M. Akram Nadwi, *al-Muḥaddithāt: the Women Scholars in Islam* (Oxford: Interface Publications, 2nd revised edn., 2013.)

1 *Naṣīḥah* means sincere advice meant to benefit the one(s) to whom it is given. Ibn Ḥazm is arguing that the Prophet's *naṣīḥah* commending the effort to come to the mosque must be commending what is to the women's benefit.

2 ʿAbd al-Razzāq, *Muṣannaf*, *Ṣalāh*, b. *shuhūd al-nisāʾ al-jamāʿah*. In another narration (see Ibn Abī Shaybah, *Muṣannaf*, *Ṣalāh*, b. *fī al-rajul yaʾummu al-nisāʾ*), Hishām ibn ʿUrwah narrates from his father: "ʿUmar ibn al-Khaṭṭāb made for the people two readers in Ramaḍān, so my father used to lead the men, and Ibn Abī Ḥathmah used to lead the women.'

attend the prayer in the mosque and ʿUmar said to her: "By God, you certainly know that I do not like this. Upon this she said: By God, I will not stop until you stop me. ʿUmar said: Then, I certainly do not stop you." When ʿUmar was attacked with the dagger she was in the mosque.[1]

ʿAlī (Ibn Ḥazm) says: the Commander of the Believers would not have stopped himself from forbidding her to go to the mosque had he known there is no reward for her in it. So then what if he had known that it decreases her reward and destroys her (good) action? There is no argument for them in his saying 'I do not like that', because there is no sin in the inclination of the self. God has known that every Muslim, had the fear of God, Exalted is He, not been (in him), he would have loved to eat when feeling hunger in Ramaḍān, and to drink when feeling thirst, and to sleep in cold mornings during the short nights abstaining from the prayer, and to have relation with every beautiful girl that the man sees. So the man loves the forbidden thing, and there is no harm on him (in that), and he is not able to turn his heart from it. What matters is only his patience or action. He says, Exalted is He:

---

1 al-Bukhārī, *Ṣaḥīḥ*, *Jumūʿah* (no chapter heading); ʿAbd al-Razzāq, *Muṣannaf*, *Ṣalāh*, b. *shuhūd al-nisāʾ al-jamāʿah*; Ibn Abī Shaybah, *Muṣannaf*, *Ṣalāh*, b. *man rakhkhaṣa li-l-nisāʾ fī al-khurūj ilā al-masjid*. The wording in *Ṣaḥīḥ al-Bukhārī* is: "A wife of ʿUmar used to attend the prayers of *fajr* and *ʿishāʾ* in the congregation in the mosque. It was said to her: Why do you go out when you know that ʿUmar does not like that, and he feels jealous? She said: Then what stops him from forbidding me? It was said to her: What stops him is the saying of the Messenger of God, upon him be peace, "Do not stop women slaves of God from the mosques of God'." In this there is a strong warning for all those who spread the false allegation that ʿUmar forbade women from going to the mosque.

"Fighting has been enjoined upon you while it is hateful to you. But perhaps you hate a thing and it is good for you; and perhaps you love a thing and it is bad for you."[1]

(140) And it has been narrated to us by the route of ʿAbd al-Razzāq, from Muḥammad ibn ʿUmārah, from ʿAmr al-Thaqafī, from ʿArfajah, that: "ʿAlī ibn Abī Ṭālib used to command the people to do night prayer in Ramaḍān, then he would make an imām for the men and an imām for the women. He commanded me (ʿArjafah) so I led the women in the prayer.'[2]

(No difference between young and old women in this regard)

ʿAlī (Ibn Hazm) says: the young women and other than them are equal.[3]

And from God, Exalted is He, is the help to being right.

1 Qurʾān, *al-Baqarah*, 2:216.

2 ʿAbd al-Razzāq, *Muṣannaf*, *Ṣalāh*, b. *shuhūd al-nisāʾ al-jamāʿah*; Ibn Abī Shaybah, *Muṣannaf*, *Ṣalāh*, b. *fī al-rajul yaʾummu al-nisāʾ*.

3 Ibn Ḥazm here rebuts the view that elderly women may go to the mosques, but young women not. The Prophet, upon him be peace, made no such distinction. Rather, he encouraged even the young girls to attend the *ʿīd*s. Similarly, the caliphs after him never stopped young women from going to the mosque.

Questions and answers: Synopsis

Questions and answers

The questions put to me by readers of the earlier edition of this book were (with the exception of the fourth, below) taken up in that edition. I have to accept that they were not dealt with in a way satisfactory to all. I take this opportunity to lay out the matter more fully, accepting the risk of repetition. I address the questions separately, then what they have in common, and end with some general thoughts about the relation between *sunnah*s and the rules of *fiqh*.

Question 1: *Encouraging women to attend prayers in the mosques seems to be motivated by the concerns of modern feminists. Will appeasing these concerns not push Muslims towards the self-centred individualism of contemporary Western culture?*

Ibn Ḥazm's argument was written too long ago for it to be fitted to modern feminist concerns. No self-respecting feminist could tolerate the assumption, explicit at many points in the Ibn Ḥazm text (and well-established in Islamic *fiqh* generally), that fathers and husbands have responsibility for the welfare of their daughters and wives, which gives them some say over their actions. The issue is only whether this say extends to forbidding the women to go out for the congregational prayers in the mosques. The teaching in the ḥadīths adduced by Ibn Ḥazm is addressed to men insofar as it is their authority, their say, that is being constrained. Viewed from this angle it is hard to see how his argument could be connected to any feminist drive for 'agency', for 'empowering' women to move into public spaces hitherto reserved by men exclusively for themselves.

However, the Prophet did not merely forbid men to forbid women from going to the mosques. We know for certain that he commended women to go to the mosques for the prayers. He made that easier for them by arranging a separate entrance for them. We also know for certain that this practice was sustained by his Companions during and after his lifetime, even if some of them wished he had not commanded that. This positive side of the *sunnah* in question has important implications – as we shall come to, below – for women's active presence in the mosque space, their visibility and audibility there on behalf of their responsibility for the religion.

Neglect of this *sunnah* (for the best or worst of motives) is a factor in the web of arrangements in Muslim societies that have combined, over time, to diminish the status, dignity and agency of Muslim women. That should interest anyone concerned about the injustices and other harms that flow from denying women the respect due to them. However, the cultural idiom of the discussion (above and below) will not have much appeal to feminists schooled in the contemporary Western understanding of human nature. This understanding claims that the difference between male and female is not significant in the overall development of human personality and character, and so ought not to be the basis of discrimination in any sphere of life. The traditional social and cultural boundaries (e.g., different parenting roles, gender differences) are 'constructs' that exploit the physical differences in favour of the stronger sex. The story of this exploitation is complicated and entails women being passive or complicit in accepting social and political disadvantage. Hence the aggressive tone of some feminist campaigners to undo the disadvantage, even while they insist on material support from husbands and/or the state for themselves and their children. This is not the place to go into the variants of feminism, or to counter-argue in favour of the relevance to the development of human personality, will, conscience and character of the traditional role boundaries. What I have said is sufficient to indicate that my presentation of Ibn Ḥazm's argument would have been intellectually dishonest if it claimed that he somehow intended or wished to shift those role boundaries. No. His argument is strictly and narrowly positioned within, and on behalf of, the Prophetic *sunnah* in respect of women's presence in the mosques.

Question 2: *If it is as important for women as it is for men to attend congregational prayers in the mosque, why is it not required of women that they do so, as it is required of men?*

It is the case that, if there is no practical impediment to his doing so, a man must make effort to do the *farḍ* prayers in congregation, rather than individually in his home or elsewhere. It is also the case, as established from the ḥadīth, that the Prophet, upon him be peace, forbade men to forbid women to attend prayers in the mosque. He himself encouraged women to do so. His teaching also makes it abundantly clear that as regards the benefits, here and hereafter, from praying in the mosque rather than at home, there is no difference between men and women.

That said, there is consensus among jurists that it is not an emphasized *sunnah* for the women to attend *farḍ* prayers in the mosque. Ibn Ḥazm holds that it is mandatory on all men who hear the call to prayer to go to a mosque for the prayer to which the *adhān* has called them.[1] He does not consider this to be mandatory for women: "(Attending the prayer in the mosque) is not obligatory on the women but, if they do attend, then they do good and it is better for them (to do so)." The juristic consensus is supported by our firm knowledge that not all women attended prayers in the mosque during the time of the Prophet, and those who did attend did not attend them all.

The severity with which the Prophet, upon him be peace, viewed men who, without valid excuse, did not attend prayers in the mosque, is indicated by this ḥadīth from Abū Hurayrah: the Prophet said:

> The prayers hardest on the hypocrites are *ʿishāʾ* and *fajr*. If they knew what is in them (i.e., of reward) they would come to them even if they had to walk on their hips. For sure I had in mind to command the prayer to be set and a man to lead the prayer; then, accompanied by some men with piles of wood, to walk to (the houses of) those men who did not attend the prayer and set their houses on fire over them.[2]

---

1 *al-Muḥallā*, 4/188.

2 al-Bukhārī, *Ṣaḥīḥ*, *Adhān*, b. *faḍl al-ʿishāʾ fī al-jamāʿah*; Muslim, *Ṣaḥīḥ*, *Masājid wa-mawāḍiʿ al-ṣalāh*, b. *faḍl ṣalāt al-jamāʿah*.

There is no record of any similar statement about women. We can be sure that the reference to men in the *ḥadīth* does not implicitly include women because, in another version, the presence of women and children in the houses is given as the reason for not setting fire to them: "If the women and children had not been in the houses, then I would have established the prayer of *ʿishāʾ* and I would have commanded my young men to set fire to the houses."[1]

It would be a valid excuse for a man unable to leave young children or elderly or sick persons unattended, that he did not go out to the mosque in response to the call to prayer. That is typically the situation of women for long periods in their lives, and (most probably) the basis of not requiring them to do the *farḍ* prayers in the mosque. It is not practical to require that they make arrangements to be able to leave the house five times a day, in order to respond to the *adhān*. By contrast, since men are not typically in the role of carers of those who can no longer, or who cannot yet, take care of themselves, they are expected to arrange their affairs so as to be able to do the *farḍ* prayers in the mosque.

The reason for not commanding women to do that is (most likely) the nature and persistence of their typical everyday preoccupations. Such a command could engender resentment either toward the command or toward the preoccupations or both. The point of nevertheless holding to the commendation is that the desire to attend the mosques, a major factor in preserving the prayers and the moral standing of the community, should be felt just as keenly by women as it should be by men. Both are answerable for the norms of the community they are

---

1 Aḥmad ibn Ḥanbal, *Musnad*, *musnad Abī Hurayrah*.

part of. Norms can be helped by rulings but the two are not the same, a matter I shall return to.

Question 3: *Did ᶜUmar not stop women from attending prayers in the mosques?*

This allegation is false, without basis in even the weakest reports. It is nevertheless repeated in many contexts. The reason for that here must be to find, through the example of ᶜUmar, some legitimacy for avoiding this particular *sunnah*. Among Sunnis ᶜUmar is an exceptionally revered figure. In part this is because the heartlands of Islam were defined, territorially and administratively, under his leadership. But in greater part it is because he was a close confidant of the Prophet, upon him be peace, from the earliest years of revelation, and after that a champion of his Sunnah. He applied it strictly, without fear or favour, against members of his own close kin, and the elite among the Companions, no matter how popular they had become. If it could be credibly asserted that such a man forbade women from praying in the mosques, it might excuse others refusing the *sunnah* as impracticable or contrary to the public interest.

However, as unmistakably demonstrated by the soundest of reports, ᶜUmar never forbade women in general to go to the mosques, nor any individual woman, not even his own wife, despite personal feelings about her doing so.

Furthermore, ᶜUmar's practice on this matter is consistent with other elements of his policy. He did not oppose the presence, the visibility or audibility, of women in the public domain generally. For example, it is he who appointed al-Shifāʾ bint

ʿAbdillāh to supervise the market of Madinah, the Muslims' capital city at that time.[1] During his rule women, while under no religious obligation to do so, participated actively in the military jihād in al-Shām (Greater Syria) and elsewhere.[2] Also, his verbal encounters with women in the mosque are well known. On one occasion, he was challenged while he was giving a *khuṭbah* in which he counselled limiting the size of dowries, so as to reduce the burden on men. A woman in the congregation said to him: "O Commander of the Believers, God's Book is more worthy to be followed (than you). God has said: *If you have given one of them (i.e., women) abundant wealth, then do not take it back*."[3] In response, ʿUmar said: "ʿUmar made a mistake and the woman is right."[4]

Question 4: *Is it not the case that women came to the mosque primarily to listen to the Prophet's teaching, not to attend the prayers?*

No. This bizarre opinion (held, I am told, by an *ʿālim* in India) is false in light of the many sound ḥadīths that women attended the mosque for the prayers. Some of them were presented earlier. In one, ʿĀʾishah reports (as do several other narrators) an occasion when the Prophet, upon him be peace, was so late coming out for the *ʿishāʾ* prayer that ʿUmar called out: "The women and children have fallen asleep..."

---

1 Abū Nuʿaym al-Aṣbahānī, *Maʿrifat al-ṣaḥābah*, 5/261.

2 See Saʿīd ibn Manṣūr, *Sunan*, *Jihād*, b. *mā jāʾa fī suhmān al-nisāʾ*.

3 Qurʾān, *al-Nisāʾ*, 4:20.

4 Saʿīd ibn Manṣūr, *Sunan*, ḥadīth no. 598; al-Bayhaqī, *al-Sunan al-kubrā*, 7/233.

They were not waiting in the mosque to hear a sermon as the Prophet did not give sermons so late in the night. It is also reliably reported that the Prophet would remain seated after the *salām* (marking the end of the prayer) and ask the men to do the same so that the women could leave the mosque first. If they had only been there to hear him teach, they would not leave the assembly directly after the *salām*. Then there is the detailed *fiqh* about the men's and women's rows – a needless effort if it were never expected that women may attend, in the same place, the prayers that men attend.

I cannot see any way in which this opinion can be made to seem reasonable. Perhaps the scholar holding it thinks that women's going to the mosque was an arrangement special to the lifetime of the Prophet and, after his decease, suspended – after all, this was a unique opportunity to be in the presence of the Messenger of God. But this does not fit at all with the known history of the time after the Prophet. Finally, using attendance at the prayers as a ruse to get the women to listen to the Prophet's teaching – to say nothing of using a ruse at all, still less with prayers as the lure – does not fit with the well-attested fact that the Prophet reserved a day for teaching the women, separately from the men.

Question 5: *If the issue is between women's praying in the mosques being commended and its being merely permitted, why does the title of this book use the word 'lawfulness'?*

Because, as I explained in the Preface of the first edition, our lived reality is that, in some communities, women are actually turned away from mosques, as if it were unlawful for them to enter. I wanted to draw attention to that reality, and take a first step that, less likely to be opposed in principle (even if ignored in practice), may open hearts and minds for the next step. That said, I should emphasize that if 'merely permitted' is believed to be the *sunnah* when in reality it is not, 'merely permitted' is bound, over time and under the influence of other factors, to acquire the meaning 'permitted to some under some conditions' (for example, to older women, not the young), and then 'not really permitted'.

Misbelief about a Prophetic *sunnah*, or misapplication or passive neglect of it, just like a consciously willed refusal of it, leads Muslims (individually and as a community) out of the circle of protection from error that is the special privilege of God's Messengers. Exposition of how that is so cannot be loaded onto a discussion of the text of Ibn Ḥazm presented here. It belongs in a discussion of alterations or additions to the religion (*bidaʿa*), which is best attempted separately.

Question 6: *If you are convinced that women's being commended to pray in the mosques is the sunnah, and this sunnah is neglected, why take such a cautious approach to restoring it? Why a quiet, private campaign and not a vocal, public one?*

Assuming this question has to do with appropriate tactics, there is a short answer to it:

In the mainstream Sunni tradition, it is well understood that means and ends must both be lawful, not only the ends. If, in a given situation, predictable outcomes of the means used include harms greater than the intended good, then it is unlikely that using those means is lawful. If mosques that refuse entry to women were to be picketed and leafleted by protesters insisting on their 'Islamic legal right' to pray in those mosques, the reaction is predictable: incivilities, hardening of attitudes, counter-attacks. The space meant to provide the community with refuge from the day's business, a space for peaceful assembly and prayer, for religious education and reflection, will become a focus of intra-communal contention. Moreover, if that contention yields a victory for either side, rancour will infest the community since any contention that has winners must also have losers.

By contrast, building consensus through example and persuasion of one or a few persons at a time, for as long as it takes, is an appropriate and effective means that does not risk the harm of fracturing an already fractious community even more. It allows people the time they need to realize that their primary loyalty should be to the Prophet's Sunnah, not to customs that, however long they have been established, work against it.

Question 7: *Ibn Ḥazm championed the fiqh of a minority school that faded out. The translated text and your notes confirm that Ḥanafī and Mālikī jurists took a different line on this issue. Why follow Ibn Ḥazm in preference to established rulings in the far more popular schools with a far larger geographical spread?*

There should be no question of 'loyally following' Ibn Ḥazm or, for that matter, Imāms Mālik or Abū Ḥanifāh or Ibn Ḥanbal, or any other great *ʿālim*. Insofar as that is permissible it is only on account of their reputation for 'loyally following' the Sunnah. It is God's Messenger, upon him be peace, whom Muslims strive to love and obey, because his religious authority is affirmed by God and God's clear command is to accept that authority ("hear and obey"), not to challenge or oppose it. This is safe to do because in all matters of belief, attitude, will, resolve, action, etc., intended to bring one more near to God, the Prophet's judgments were supported and guided by God. No human individual or institution after him can be accorded this status. Religious authority is safe from error only because, and to the extent that, it follows what has been reliably transmitted of the Prophet's Sunnah. On the same lines, the community of Muslims as a whole (not any one lineage, or city, or institution within it) is safe from error, as the Prophet gave assurance that it would be, only because there will be, in all times, individual voices (in the present case, Ibn Ḥazm) who derive judgments and give counsel on the basis of conscientious enquiry into the Prophetic *sunnah*, not on the basis of what may be easier for the majority in a given time and place because nearer to their customs, nor on the basis of what is in conformity with the rulings of one's school.

On any particular issue, insofar as it can be isolated from related issues, there is safety only in following what is closest to the *sunnah*, if the reports demonstrating it are sound and their meaning clear enough to be understood and acted upon. On the question of whether it is commendable or merely permissible for women to do the congregational prayers in the mosque, the proof-texts and argument put forward by Ibn Ḥazm are much stronger than the positions eventually adopted in the schools named after Mālik and Abū Ḥanīfah.

On the personal credibility of Ibn Ḥazm with his intellectual peers, see above, Introduction. As for the popularity and geographical spread of one school relative to another: the principal determining factor is more directly associated with the historical ups-and-downs of political power than with the virtues of doctrines and methods. The Ḥanafī school is the largest mainly because it was favoured by the Ottoman and Mughal dynasties who ruled for a long time over extensive and populous territories. The eventual displacement of the Ẓāhirī school by the Mālikī school may, similarly, be explained by the support for the latter of the dynasties that came to power in the western parts of the Islamic world. No doubt, greater adaptability of method may have made one school more attractive to political regimes than another. But the main factor was networks of mutual dependence between regimes and schools as they rose to power and strove to maintain it.

The question deserves more detailed consideration than I can give it here. For the issue in hand, what is decisive for the weight of religious authority is direct, near-to-hand and clear adherence to the *sunnah*, which is evident in the exposition of it by Ibn Ḥazm. His 'identity' as a Ẓāhirī is not relevant for a decision as to the rightness of his argument.

Question 8: *How and why did the mainstream schools of Sunnī fiqh adopt the view that it is preferable for women to pray in their homes?*

In answering this question I address mainly Ḥanafī *fiqh*, in part because this *fiqh* is the most widespread worldwide; and in part because those who raise the question are of South Asian ancestry and therefore predominantly of the Ḥanafī school.

The argument of Ibn Ḥazm is that the Prophet, upon him be peace, invited and encouraged women to attend daily prayers in the mosque, as also the Friday prayer and the prayers on the two *ʿīd*s, and to come to the mosque so that they, like the men, could hear him teach the right understanding and practice of Islam. One effect of this *sunnah* was that by attending the Prophet's mosque women became aware of their obligation to acquire knowledge of Islam from him directly, as the men did. During his lifetime, and for most of the rule of the rightly guided caliphs, women came to the mosques for prayers and other gatherings in enough numbers and with enough regularity for this practice to be widespread, in Madinah and other cities, so that it was never questioned (even after the practice fell into disuse) as something doubtful, let alone undesirable. Women even did *iʿtikāf* in the mosques; ʿĀʾishah's doing so after the death of the Prophet is recorded by Imām Mālik.[1] When doing the *tarāwīḥ* in congregation during Ramaḍān became established – these prayers, also known as *qiyām al-layl* or night prayer, are not obligatory – provision was made for women. ʿUmar ibn al-Khaṭṭāb appointed Sulaymān ibn Abī Ḥathmah to lead the women's assembly at the back of the mosque.[2] ʿAlī ibn Abī Ṭālib also urged attendance at the night prayers of Ramaḍān, appointed an imām for the men's congregation and an imām for the women's.[3]

When the *ummah* was tested by dissensions and civil war (*fitan*; sing. *fitnah*), the region worst affected was Iraq, and within Iraq the city of Kufah. Here the Khawārij, the Shīʿa

---

1 Mālik, *al-Muwaṭṭā*, b. *dhikr al-iʿtikāf.*

2 al-Kattānī, Muḥammad ibn al-Muntaṣir, *Muʿjam fiqh al-salaf*, 2/130.

3 ʿArfajah ibn ʿAbdullāh al-Thaqafī says: "He (ʿAlī) appointed me to lead the women in prayer." al-Kattānī, Muḥammad ibn al-Muntaṣir, *Muʿjam fiqh al-salaf*, 2/130.

and others plotted raids and rebellions and engaged in fierce propaganda on behalf of their respective sects and factions. In so doing, all factions neglected the Qurʾānic command to refer disputes to the judgement of God and His Messenger and thereafter live peaceably, deferring any differences that remained to the divine arbitration hereafter. This dissension lasted, with ups and downs in intensity, through the Umayyad period and the early phase of ʿAbbāsid rule, i.e., through most of the first half of the second century after the Hijrah.

Kufah became the breeding-ground of the most vigorous factionalism, attracting recruits to extremist ideas and sending them out to other territories. Part of the reason was the city's mixture of (formerly feuding) tribes of Arabs from the Peninsula, and a fast-growing non-Arab population. The latter carried into their understanding of Islam the legacy of the ancient Persian and Greek-Roman empires. The military victory of the Muslims overturned the political power, but not the intellectual and cultural prestige, that these empires enjoyed in the region. The non-Arab converts were able to reformulate their conceptions about God, about sacred scripture, about prophets, saints and sages, using some of the language of Qurʾān and Sunnah. They did this with a confident sophistication that must have impressed and troubled the Arabs of the early generations of Arab Muslims. There is agreement among historians that the development of method and doctrines in 'Islamic theology' owed a lot to the learned elite among non-Arab converts. Their predictably unresolvable debates led to ever more elaborate rationalizations till, in the end, people were producing formal creeds *(ʿaqīda*s*)* to proclaim the distinctive rightness of their faction relative to another, which helped aggravate rather than heal the divisions among factions. A comparable influence from non-Arab cultures can be discerned in matters to do with social relations, notably the place in society of men and women, and this, as we see below, affected the development of *fiqh* on these matters.

(It is worth pausing here to recall that the brilliant efforts of Muslims, Arab and non-Arab, to remember and record the teachings of the Prophet, must have been motivated by the will to derive Islamic values from his authority before giving any thought to any other source, just as the Qurʾān commanded. They must have intended to secure thereby the unity of the religion, its norms and laws, and its adherents. If Muslims have enjoyed a substantial degree of shared identity of life-ways and manners across the boundaries of times, regions and cultures, it is owed to the efforts of the men and women who in person studied, and in person taught, the corpus of Prophetic ḥadīth, not as an abstract ideal but as a rule of daily life, demonstrable in their own practice. We owe a huge debt to these devout men and women, and should not be niggardly in acknowledging it.)

The *fiqh* that developed in Kufah developed in the context of the civil and intellectual strife in the city. Women, when coming out to attend the mosques, especially in the hours of darkness, may have faced the threat of harassment, even abduction. In addition, there were concerns about the comportment of men and women when they assembled at the mosques. In those days, there was no physical barrier in the prayer space between the men's rows and the women's, nor were there separated spaces for doing the necessary ablutions. Rather, men and women would have been able to see and hear each other, just as they did in the market-place. Hence the importance of the Qurʾānic instructions to both men and women, in situations where they encounter each other, to "lower their gaze" (meaning that they should not try to look for, in each other, the kind of interest that can lead to flirtation); since women have more equipment to do that with, and perhaps also more need to be noticed and appreciated, the instructions to them regarding dress and comportment are more detailed. Though it is not spelled out, some concerns about the intentions with which men and women assembled and how they behaved in and around the mosque were in ʿĀʾishah's mind when she complained (in the sound ḥadīth that Ibn Ḥazm discussed at such length) about the 'new thing' that women were doing in Madinah.

In Kufah, the *fiqh* that later became the Ḥanafī school, emerged out of the rulings of the eminent Companion, ʿAbdullāh ibn Masʿūd. He said: "No woman has prayed a prayer better than praying in her house except that she prays at the sacred mosque, but an elderly woman praying in unattractive clothes."[1] Ibn Masʿūd exhorted women to pray in the home but he did not forbid them from coming to the mosque. That is why many women, notably his own wife, continued praying in the mosque. Ibrāhīm al-Nakhaʿī (d. 96, the most important of the teachers of Abū Ḥanīfah's own teachers) narrates that the wife of Ibn Masʿūd used to pray *ʿishāʾ* (i.e., after dark) in Kufah's congregational mosque.[2]That Ibn Masʿūd accepted the right of women to pray in the mosque is clear from his detailed discussion on how to arrange the women's rows in accordance with the Prophetic *sunnah*. He is reported to have

1 Ibn Abī Shaybah, *al-Muṣannaf*, 5/201. Word for word, the Arabic says "except for an old woman praying in old footwear".

2 Ibn Abī Shaybah, *al-Muṣannaf*, 5/200.

said: "For women, the best row is the last one",[1] whereas for men it is the other way around. He also said that older women should form the first row and younger women the last.[2] The reason is, most probably, that women would then more easily restrain their desire or need to be seen and appreciated, which is naturally stronger in younger women, and therefore be better able to keep their attention on the purpose of going to the mosque. As for the men, the further they are from the younger women, the less temptation not to "lower their gaze".

Elsewhere in Iraq, women continued to go to the mosques, while most jurists (probably on grounds of safety) disapproved their going to mosques far from their own quarter. Ḥasan al-Baṣrī was asked about a woman who vowed that if her husband were released from prison she would pray two *rakʿah*s in every congregational mosque in Basrah. He said: "She should pray in the mosque of her people." He added that ʿUmar would have been severe with her for making such a vow.[3]

During the governorship of al-Ḥajjāj (75–95), *fitnah* intensified and jurists became even more circumspect about women going out to the mosque. Ibrāhīm al-Nakhaʿī did not permit his wives to go out for *jumūʿah* or any other congregational prayer in the mosque.[4] The transition from Umayyad to ʿAbbāsid rule was marked by a lot of bloodshed, and greater protectiveness towards women. Sufyān al-Thawrī (d. 161) says: "There is nothing better for the woman than her

1 Ibn Abī Shaybah, *al-Muṣannaf*, 5/204.
2 Ibn Abī Shaybah, *al-Muṣannaf*, 5/204.
3 Ibn Abī Shaybah, *al-Muṣannaf*, 5/202.
4 Ibn Abī Shaybah, *al-Muṣannaf*, 5/204.

house even if she is old."[1] Imām Abū Ḥanīfah (d. 150) lived through this period, and hence he too discouraged women from attending the mosques. His famous students Abū Yūsuf (d. 182) and Muḥammad al-Shaybānī (d. 181), living in the more peaceful time after the ʿAbbāsid caliphate was secure, relaxed the rulings of their teacher on this matter a little. But, by this time, there had been a noticeable change in the underlying reasons for the rulings, strict or relaxed.

Al-Kāsānī (d. 587, author of one of the most succinct, professional compendia of Ḥanafī *fiqh*) affirms that Ḥanafī jurists are agreed that it is not allowed for young women to go out to attend the *jumūʿah* prayer, *ʿīd* prayer or any other prayer. Their reasoning is that young women's going out is a *fitnah*, the word here meaning 'temptation'. Now it appears – as any contemporary feminists will be quick to remark – that the ruling has less to do with the protection *of* women than with protection of men *from* women. Perhaps contemporary feminists (because such rulings are being issued by men to manage the movements of women) are not giving sufficient attention to the possibility that these rulings may also be intended to protect women from themselves, so that the motive for attending the prayers is not confounded by any indulgence of the desire or need to be seen and appreciated. Al-Kāsānī clarifies that there is no difference of opinion that older women are allowed to go out (in the hours of darkness) for *fajr*, *maghrib*, *ʿishāʾ* prayers, or to join the large crowds of worshippers at the *ʿīd* prayers. There is a difference as to their attendance of *ẓuhr*, *ʿaṣr* and *jumūʿah* prayers. He notes that Abū Ḥanīfah does not permit them even this much while

1 Ibn ʿAbd al-Barr, k. *al-Istidhkār*, b. *mā jāʾa fī khurūj al-nisāʾ ilā al-masājid*.

Abū Yūsuf and Muḥammad do.[1] Abū Yūsuf said: "There is no harm for an older woman to go out for all the prayers, and I disapprove that for a young woman."[2]

The change in the reasoning behind the discouragement of women's attending the mosques is not the result of ignorance of what the *sunnah* allows. No scholar in this period went so far as to forbid women from attending the prayers in the mosques or actively campaigned to stop them doing so. For example, Ibn al-Mubārak (d. 181) said: "At the present time I don't approve that women go out for *ʿīd* prayers; but if the woman insists then her husband should allow her (to go)."[3] Abū Ḥanīfah himself did not deny the right of women to pray in congregation in the mosques. He was well informed of the relevant *sunnah* and had it in mind when he discusses how they should arrange the rows in the mosques, and also what is the case if it happens in some odd circumstance that a woman is standing next to the men in their rows. The last point is worth reflecting on in some detail:

Muḥammad al-Shaybānī records in *al-Aṣl*: "I said (to Abū Ḥanīfah): What is your opinion regarding a woman who prays with the people in the row and she is praying the same prayer as the imām, following him (as the men are doing)? What is her state and the state of the men next to her? He said: Her prayer is complete, and also the prayer of all of the people is complete, except the man who is on her right, the man who is on her left, and the man who is directly behind her.

---

1 For the details, see al-Kāsānī, *Badāʾiʿ al-sanāʾiʿ*, 2/237–9.

2 Ibn ʿAbd al-Barr, k. *al-Istidhkār*, b. *mā jāʾa fī khurūj al-nisāʾ ilā al-masājid.*

3 Ibn ʿAbd al-Barr, k. *al-Istidhkār*, b. *mā jāʾa fī khurūj al-nisāʾ ilā al-masājid.*

These three men have to repeat the prayer. I asked: Why? He answered: Because these three men have served to shield the men behind them (from any distraction), and each of them is like a wall between the woman and his companions (i.e., the other men praying the same prayer behind the same imām)."[1]

Muḥammad says: "I asked: What is your opinion regarding a woman praying next to a man the same prayer, but each of them is praying their prayer separately (i.e., not as a congregation)? He said: The prayer of both is complete."[2]

Muḥammad says: "I asked him concerning a man and a woman who missed one *rakʿah* with the imam; when the imam finished the prayer, both stood up to do their missed *rakʿah*, one standing next to the other: does the woman invalidate the man's prayer? He answered: No."[3]

In each of these cases, the common notion is that a man can be distracted by a woman praying either beside or directly in front of him only if he has to keep in mind aligning his movement in the prayer with her movement. If they are moving separately (for example when praying a *rakʿah* of the congregational prayer that has been missed), the man does not have the woman's movement in mind and so his prayer is deemed "complete". The proximity of a man in no circumstance diminishes the prayer of a woman.

Abū Ḥanīfah's answers to his student's questions indicate a realistic grasp of the relative affect on men, while in prayer, of thinking about women. He ruled accordingly. There is not the slightest trace in his rulings of anything resembling the notion that the presence of women is, in and of itself,

1 Muḥammad al-Shaybānī, *al-Aṣl*, 1/161–2.

2 Muḥammad al-Shaybānī, *al-Aṣl*, 1/163.

3 Muḥammad al-Shaybānī, *al-Aṣl*, 1/164.

inherently corruptive, either generally or specifically for the effort of prayer. Neither Abū Ḥanīfah nor any other of the great imāms of *fiqh*, all of whom tried to model their thoughts and actions on what had reached them of the Prophet's teaching, refused that teaching or distorted it in order to suit the material conditions, conventions or tastes of the times in which they lived.

However, as the generations passed, as *fiqh* became consolidated, institutionalised and professionalised in distinct schools, the habit of reference back to the Book of God and the example of His Messenger weakened until it was practically replaced by reference to legal precedents in the school. The rulings of the *fuqahā*ʾ came to be regarded as direct sources of authoritative guidance on how to imagine and embody Islam in everyday life. In practice, if never in principle, the Sunnah was neglected, and thinking about these matters became corrupted by concepts and tastes of non-Muslim provenance. As we have seen, among even the generation of the Companions, there were individual men who were determined to refuse the teaching of the Prophet when it came to 'controlling' when and where their women could go. Among the Arabs there was resentment also about the rights of property and inheritance that Muslim women were now supposed to enjoy, which gave them some measure of dignity, if not independence, from men. Among non-Arab converts, there were intellectual traditions of high pedigree that doubted the rationality of women; ascetic (gnostic and philosophical) traditions that regarded women as by nature immersed in the gross, fleshly materiality of the world, a necessity for reproduction but a fearful temptation that should be avoided because prejudicial to any hope of spiritual progress; and religious traditions which required that women be silent, as if absent, during the celebration of formal rites, and which denied women authority to officiate on behalf of the religion because they were women.

I am sure that readers will easily recognise the traces of these ideas in the evolution of practice in the matter of women attending prayers in the mosque.

Kufah was a special case on account of its having been, in the early centuries, a centre of major political and sectarian troubles. These *fitnah*s are reflected in many aspects of Ḥanafī *fiqh*. Later this school spread, in different times, to different regions of the world where the conditions were not as they had been where its *fiqh* originated. But the later jurists stuck to those early, strict opinions about women attending the prayers in the mosques. They discouraged women so much that in some places, for example South Asia, it became unimaginable that women should attend any prayer in a mosque. Ḥanafī school texts remained firmly on these same early positions, even though the conditions of that period no longer applied. This is a sign that the *fiqh* had replaced the *sunnah* as a point of reference. I quote a few rulings here from al-Kāsānī's (d. 587) *Badāʾiʿ al-sanāʾiʿ* to illustrate this:

Al-Kāsānī mentions that when there are men, children and women in the prayer, the men will stand behind the imām, then the children, then the women. He also says that if there is only one woman beside the imām, she should stand behind the imām (rather than next to him, as would be the case for a congregation of two men).[1]

He holds that it is not obligatory for women to attend prayers in congregation, because there is *fitnah* in their

1 al-Kāsānī, *Badaʾiʿ al-sanaʾiʿ*, 1/678–9.

going out to join in the congregations.[1] He also states that it is not permissible for young women to go out to attend congregational prayers.[2]

He says that a congregation is minimally constituted by one person other than the imām, and it is the same whether this one other is a man, or a woman, or a child who has reached the age of understanding.[3]

He holds that a woman is qualified to lead the prayer in general, and if she leads other women she should stand in the middle of the row, because it has been narrated that ᶜĀʾishah and Umm Salamah led other women in the prayer in this way, i.e., they did not stand out ahead of the other worshippers. He remarks that a women-only congregation is disliked "by us" (i.e., the Ḥanafīs), while it is considered commendable according to Imām Shāfiᶜī.[4]

In other cities such as Makkah, or major settlements in Syria, and later in Baghdad, the *fitnah* argument did not have the same weight as it had in Kufah. However, there was some impact from this thinking. For example, ᶜAbdullāh ibn ᶜAbbās, like ᶜAbdullāh ibn Masᶜūd, preferred women to pray at home except for older women, and except in the sacred mosques.[5] Even so, they would not stop women from going to the mosques. They too discussed the arrangement of women's rows in the mosques. ᶜAṭāʾ ibn Abī Rabāḥ said: a woman is a

1 al-Kāsānī, *Badaʾiᶜ al-sanaʾiᶜ*, 1/663.
2 al-Kāsānī, *Badaʾiᶜ al-sanaʾiᶜ*, 1/668.
3 al-Kāsānī, *Badaʾiᶜ al-sanaʾiᶜ*, 1/665.
4 al-Kāsānī, *Badaʾiᶜ al-sanaʾiᶜ*, 1/668.
5 Ibn Abī Shaybah, *al-Muṣannaf*, 5/201–2.

row.[1] While the Shāfiʿī and Ḥanbalī schools preferred women to pray at home, they nevertheless allowed them to pray in the mosques. In those regions where Shāfiʿī and Ḥanbalī *madhhab*s have been strong, women have continued to attend the mosques. Some of the chapter headings in the *Ṣaḥīḥ* of Ibn Khuzaymah (d. 311), who in general followed Shāfiʿī opinion, make this clear: the 'permissibility of setting up a tent or huts for women in the mosque'; 'the permissibility of women's going out for both *ʿīd*s whether they are virgins, unmarried, and whether they are in menstruation or pure'; 'permissibility of women doing *iʿtikāf* in the congregational mosques with their husbands when they are doing *iʿtikāf*.'

Madinah was the city of the Prophet, where his teachings were applied under his own supervision, and where rightly guided caliphs made sure that his practice was respected as authoritative and followed. Accordingly, Madinan jurists generally allowed women to attend the prayers in the mosque. They too discussed how to arrange their rows. Abū Hurayrah said: "The best row of the women is the last one, and the worst is the first one."[2] To ʿUrwah ibn Zubayr likewise is attributed the same saying in the same words.[3]

As for Imām Mālik's opinion, Ibn al-Qāsim narrated that Mālik said: "The women should not be stopped from going to the mosques."[4] Ashhab narrated from Mālik that he said: "The old woman may go out to the mosque without walking around much. The young woman may go out (to the mosque)

---

1 Ibn Abī Shaybah, *al-Muṣannaf*, 5/184.

2 Ibn Abī Shaybah, *al-Muṣannaf*, 5/204.

3 Ibn Abī Shaybah, *al-Muṣannaf*, 5/204.

4 Ibn ʿAbd al-Barr, k. *al-Itidhkār*, b. *mā jāʾa fī khurūj al-nisāʾ ilā al-masājid.*

occasionally."[1] Evidently, Imām Mālik did not intend women to exclude themselves from the mosques just because they were women; his concern was, as it should be, with the effect of their presence on their own prayers and on those of others. He allowed, if such a need arose, for a woman in *iᶜtikāf* to contract a marriage in the mosque where she was, so long as she did not have intimate relations.[2]

In modern times, most jurists in most Muslim societies do not forbid women to attend the prayers in the mosques. The scholars of or from South Asia are still reluctant to do the same, but even among them the attitude is beginning to shift. It is a pleasure for me to note that in northern England where, just two years ago, women were turned away from mosques, they are now allowed to use the mosques during the day, i.e., when they are away from home and need somewhere to do their prayers. This is a very small step indeed, but a step in the right direction.

What these Questions have in common

Each of the questions summarily answered above implies some degree of disbelief that the *sunnah* really is that women, if they can, should do the obligatory prayers in the mosques, i.e., that their presence in the mosques is not just tolerable and permissible but commendable without being (as is the case for men) all but mandatory.

A Prophetic *sunnah* is established in accordance with well-known criteria: its being in agreement with the clear meaning

1 Ibn ᶜAbd al-Barr, k. *al-Itidhkār*, b. *mā jāʾa fī khurūj al-nisāʾ ilā al-masājid.*

2 *Malik*, *al-Muwaṭṭā*, b. *al-nikāḥ fī al-iᶜtikāf.*

of the Qurʾān; the soundness of the ḥadīths adduced as proof-texts for it; the centrality of those ḥadīths (i.e., their being reported widely, without interruption from the earliest period; their recognition by specialists in *fiqh* as relevant for the matter in question; their agreeing with each other in general meaning and important details); and the consensus about them in the discourse and practice of the Prophet's Companions and those who followed them in striving to preserve the Sunnah.

A *sunnah* is not established by an unusual ḥadīth, one divergent from other ḥadīths on the same or similar issues. Nor is a *sunnah* established by a weak *(ḍaʿīf)* ḥadīth, whose reporter(s) or transmission history have been considered by ḥadīth experts to be suspect. A *sunnah* is not established on the basis of the judgement of one Companion if another is known to have disagreed. This is so even if the Companion is as eminent in the formative history of Islam as an ʿĀʾishah bint Abū Bakr or ʿUmar ibn al-Khaṭṭāb. Companion reports are definitive of a *sunnah* only when there is a consensus among them. Otherwise, they are, as with unusual or weak Prophetic ḥadīths, relevant to bear in mind, but not decisive. They are kept in mind because they can be useful either in supporting a ruling or in qualifying it – so that, for example, it may be implemented cautiously and flexibly, for greater effectiveness in different situations.

The criteria just mentioned, positive and negative, are not themselves disputed among scholars, though how well they have been applied in any particular case often is subject to dispute. In respect of Ibn Ḥazm's argument that women should be commended and encouraged to attend the prayers in the mosques, there is really no room for uncertainty as to what the *sunnah* is. In this particular case, we even have record of Companions wishing the *sunnah* were otherwise but not acting to oppose it, just as there were some (like ʿUmar's grandson, Bilāl) who knew what the *sunnah* was but were resolved to oppose it. The majority *fiqh* came to settle on the view that it is permissible for women to attend prayers in the mosques, but better for them to pray at home.

The long prevalence of that view explains the disbelief in the judgment that, despite its prevalence, it is a departure from the *sunnah*, a *bidʿah*. So, to defend it, it is said: (1) this view is inspired from outside Islam, specifically modern feminist concerns. Or (2), the matter is not clear-cut. If it were, women would, like men, have been commanded to go to the mosque for the prayers, with exemptions (more explicit and indulgent than for men) for women whose responsibilities made that impracticable. (3) Some senior figure in Islamic history (an ʿUmar or an ʿĀʾishah) wanted to oppose women going to the mosque, or at least wished the practice to be allowed to lapse. (4) The texts have been misunderstood: women did not go to the mosque primarily to do the congregational prayers but to hear the Prophet's teaching. (7, 8) Ibn Ḥazm's argument is a minority view, whereas the majority schools prefer that women pray at home. If the two arguments are equally valid, it is safer to stay with the majority view. (5, 6) If the matter really were as clear-cut as claimed one should campaign for it, not ask that people take note of it and bring it to the attention of others only in ways that will not risk upsetting them.

These defences of the view that it is better for women to pray at home do not offer much by way of positive arguments based on the Sunnah. They defend it quite simply as the view accepted within the *fiqh* that prevailed over a large expanse of territory and time, i.e., as the established custom. They do not think that it is the established custom because it is right; rather, they think it is right because it is established. The scope of reference in the minds of the objectors does not accord much prominence to the Prophetic *sunnah*.

This is most evident in Question 4. It claims that the texts telling us that women were present in the mosque for the prayers should be understood to mean that they were there primarily to hear the Prophet's sermons, not to attend the prayers. This competes for irrelevance with the argument (which gave Ibn Ḥazm an opportunity to indulge his flair for sarcasm) that the Prophet urged women to attend the *ʿīd* prayers to awe his enemies by giving an impression of the multitude of the Muslims. There is no basis for this rationale in any ḥadīth or other report. Perhaps those who suggested this rationale (*ʿilla*) dragged it over from the very different context of the Prophet's instruction to older men going into battle to dye their beards lest their white hair give heart to the enemy. It illustrates the lack of discipline that must afflict human reasoning when it is more dedicated to justifying a *fiqh* ruling than preserving a *sunnah*.

The false allegation about ʿUmar (Question 3) illustrates the temptation to fabricate authority for the sake of a *fiqh* at variance with the *sunnah*.

Taking Ibn Ḥazm's argument as just one option, other options being equally valid (Question 7), is also a denial of the *sunnah* inasmuch as it is saying that the *sunnah* is not clear enough to enable us to decide between options. But the proof-texts cited by Ibn Ḥazm *are* clear, and he does not build his argument by subjecting them to far-fetched interpretation. Finally (Question 8), the relative consistency of the major schools of Sunnī *fiqh* on this issue is offered as a ground for conviction as to its being authentically Islamic guidance.

All Muslims agree that the religious authority of a *fiqh* ruling inheres in its being derived from Qurʾān and Sunnah. Its usefulness comes from its concordance with those sources while making their guidance actionable in situations not directly envisaged in them. Thus, *fiqh* is not valued for its own sake but for its serving and preserving the guidance conveyed by the Prophet, upon him peace. That is how it is supposed to be. In reality, however, it sometimes happens that the *fiqh* becomes the end or purpose, and the authority of Qurʾān and Sunnah the means supporting that end – the reverse of what is supposed to be.

The confusion of means and end is most noticeable when we see rulings based directly on texts that their proponents themselves agree are weak but which they say are consistent with some broad 'fundamental principle' or 'public benefit', which they claim to be 'generally agreed'; when we see scholars deny the reliability or relevance of texts only because or when they go against the rulings of their own school; when we see in later times, rulings elegantly summarized, reformulated and refined, and re-grouped, but only by reference to earlier rulings. In sum, as the theory and practices of *fiqh* became institutionalized, discussion came to be controlled by, and mostly confined within, the framework of the authoritative books of one school contending with the authoritative books of one or more other schools. Qurʾān and Sunnah are then mentioned mainly for the sake of good manners. They are there in the background for sure, but the foreground is taken up by the jurists' professional concerns and rivalries.

Those concerns include the need to infer general concepts from *sunnah*s about related (or apparently related) matters and, especially, to infer the *ʿilla*, the rationale, for the Prophet's response to a question or incident or situation. Why this was a special concern is obvious – it is hardly possible to extend or adapt a judgment for different circumstances without some grasp of the rationale behind the original judgment.

In some ḥadīths, the Prophet himself states a reason for approving or rebuking something (his being silent is counted as non-rebuke or tacit acceptance). But in many more, there is no explicit *ʿilla*. In the latter case, the jurist has to infer the *ʿilla* from similar judgments on similar matters, or work out the common rationale behind dissimilar judgments on apparently similar matters. Most jurists were cautious about doing this. The example mentioned just above in connection with the Prophet urging women to attend the *ʿīd* prayers is *not* typical. They were also cautious about extending rulings by analogy based on an inferred *ʿilla*. For, as is obvious, if such an *ʿilla* is used to produce a ruling, it mimics the authority of a ruling based directly on a *sunnah* without really having that authority.

As experience with, and confidence in, the procedures of such reasoning grew, the derived concepts and inferred *ʿilla*s were gathered into postulates of higher generality, even further abstracted from the *sunnah*s that the effort of *fiqh* is supposed to serve. These postulates do not take the form of rulings themselves. Rather, they are used as maxims to guide and to check the conformity of rulings within a school. We encountered earlier an example of such a maxim in the explanation of the brilliant Ḥanafī jurist al-Kāsānī for the ruling about where a woman should stand when leading the *ṣalāh* of a congregation of women, because "the state of the woman is covering". Nothing in the Qurʾān or the sound Prophetic ḥadīths could serve, directly or indirectly, as the basis for this large statement. Nevertheless, the maxim, once widely circulated within the discipline of *fiqh* of a major school of Islamic law, is bound to carry some religious weight. And so it can be used to require, in any situation excluding emergencies, self-restraint of a woman's presence or voice so that the behaviour *religiously preferred* for her, in order to be in accord with "covering", is that she stay at home and, for any business outside home, be represented by a male.

It is impractical to apply this maxim strictly in all circumstances and so it is not, nor has ever been, applied in all circumstances. Ibn Ḥazm has a good time pointing out the inconsistency of the Ḥanafī rulings that allow a woman to travel unaccompanied on a journey of less than three days, but strongly discourage her from the short walk to her local mosque (above, p. 29). As I noted in the Introduction, Ibn Ḥazm was severely harassed by his rivals in *fiqh*, and so he hits back, allowing himself to neglect the duty of compassion. Among the benefits of compassion when disagreeing with someone is that it helps one to see the sense in an opponent's position (even while affirming that it is wrong) and so learn from it. The arrangements for local neighbourhood mosques should (and do) differ from those at mosques like the ones in Makkah, Madinah and al-Quds (Jerusalem). In these mosques large numbers of worshippers are gathered for a short time, and the vast majority of them are unlikely to know each other or meet again. At local mosques, most people do know most of those coming and going, and the traffic is regular and continuous. In uneasy hearts and minds, this can give rise to anxieties and fears (of a 'new' or 'old thing'). Some jurists thought to prevent that unease by discouraging women from going because women are not obliged to go, whereas men are. That does not justify such a ruling if, as Ibn Ḥazm has shown, it goes against the *sunnah*. Nevertheless, even as an error one can make excuse for it, which is preferable to mocking it.

Such error arises because a Prophetic judgment, appropriate to the situation it is addressing, can give rise, within the procedures of *fiqh*, to an understanding of its *ʿilla* which may be incorrect. For example, women are not required to attend prayers in the mosque: is this because they are women and not men? This understanding of the *ʿilla* may then be applied to other situations for which the original judgment was not intended. (I gave an example above in my conjecture about how impressing the enemy may have come to be offered as the *ʿilla* for urging women to attend the *ʿīd* prayers.) This wider application in turn encourages reasoning to postulates that, though detached from the *sunnah*s (and from the real situations and real people that the *sunnah*s were addressing), seem to bring a number of rulings under a single rationale, such as "the state of the woman is covering". This rationale in turn frames and controls other rulings, and so the process feeds itself. Instead of a flow of effort from a *sunnah* to a *fiqh* ruling and then (if the ruling is questioned) back to the *sunnah*, the effort circulates within the rulings and books of the schools of *fiqh*. This strengthens the status and position in society of the schools; it does not necessarily strengthen the religion, nor necessarily embody the guidance of the Qurʾān and Sunnah.

I have no doubt that Ibn Ḥazm is right as to the *sunnah* on the matter of women attending congregational prayers in the mosque. He is able to see and present this so clearly in part because his Ẓāhirī method rejects many of the processes of *fiqh* – juristic analogy, preference among lawful options, informed personal judgment – that are considered by the majority schools to be both necessary and valid. Since only the Qurʾān and the judgments of God's Messengers are protected from error, reference back to them is the only safe way to cope with differences of opinion that evolved over time into settled doctrine and custom. However, the intention and manners with which this going to Qurʾān and Sunnah is attempted should not aggravate the tensions it is seeking to reconcile. It should not add to the divisions in the Community. Sunnis (*ahl al-sunnah wa-l-jamaʿah*, the people of the Sunnah and Solidarity) should not behave as if they too were a sect. That is why I do not commend public, confrontational protest on behalf of this *sunnah*. I commend only personal effort and private counsel.

To understand how this can work, we need to digress from the particular concern of the Ibn Ḥazm text and look at the more general issue: the bare historical fact that Muslims, even as they affirm the priority owed, in their religious practice, to the Prophet's Sunnah, nevertheless depart from it into alterations and additions to the religion, *bidaʿa*. Sometimes they do a *bidʿah* though well-informed of what the relevant *sunnah* is. Sometimes they do it in unwilled ignorance of that – i.e., they make the effort to know but do not find any secure knowledge. Sometimes they do *bidʿah* in a partly-willed ignorance – i.e., they make little effort to find out or, more often, they just decide what they like to do and say 'We have not heard that this is explicitly forbidden in the religion, so we deem it to be permitted.' In each of these cases, if their intention is to serve God as best they can from within the constraint of the internal and external necessities of their life, the presumption is that, as He wills, God may forgive and reward them, despite their being in error. But the community as such is not forgiven the consequences of *bidaʿa*. However well established a *bidʿah* has become, it remains a duty to rebuke it: this is what Ibn Ḥazm is trying to do. He tries to distinguish strong, mainstream ḥadīths from weak, peripheral ones; and to distinguish clear, consistent reasoning from reasoning that is muddled and inconsistent. The justification for his doing so is not to make light of the piety and intellect of the great imāms of *fiqh*, even though sometimes his tone of voice suggests a lightness of that kind. Rather, the justification is his grasp of the fundamental principle that *fiqh* cannot serve as a direct, independent or self-dependent, source of religious guidance. That dignity must be reserved for Qurʾān and Sunnah, the sources which stand above them and have priority over them.

The Sunnah: norms and rulings

Among Sunnis, there is no disagreement as to the status of the Sunnah. It has famously been called 'the second revelation' accompanying the Qurʾān, though only the Book is 'recited'. It is also identified as 'the Wisdom' in the reiterated Qurʾānic phrase "the Book and the Wisdom". The two are coupled as the means of protection at the Hour: love and obey God and love and obey His Messenger. The Sunnah is, like the Qurʾān, an offering of *raḥmah* (the mercy of God) *li-l-ʿālamīn*, to all beings, all worlds. It is concordant with the purpose of religion generally: to bring people nearer to God so that they do what pleases Him, avoid what displeases Him, and thereby become ready for the trials of the Hour. It follows from the omniscience and compassion of God that His Message and

His Messenger's exposition of it must suffice for the believers to understand and live by since it is the final revelation. All of that is implicit in the testimonies of the *shahādah*, which legally define a Muslim. The relevance of the Sunnah in the present century of Islam is no less than in its first. That relevance is not a given; it has to be earned through an effort of reflection and will – both repeatedly urged in the Qur'ān and the *ḥadīth* – to understand and then, by adhering to it, to preserve the Sunnah. Many Muslims are content with much less than that, content to belong and not to believe.

They are content with Islam as a social or legal identity. Even that is not an easy thing, given the constant pressures in modern times to conform to the life-ways by which the dominant economic system gets and keeps its dominance. Identity is in practice susceptible to dilution and variation according to different social contexts. But, whether easy or hard to keep up, identity is not susceptible to improvement. It is what it is, a social or legal fact. But the purpose of Islam, any religion, is not to provide identity; it is to educate the will so that believers strive to enact values pleasing to God. For this effort Muslims are commanded to take the *sunnah*s of the Prophet, upon him be peace, as guide and standard. When the purpose of Islam is reduced to providing a marker of collective identity (necessary as that may be to any established religion), it risks reducing the *sunnah*s from educative norms to simple rulings, from an interior aspiration to improve oneself to an exterior conformity to avoid social disapproval. A cursory acquaintance with the Qur'ān and *ḥadīth* is enough to know that very little of the teaching of either is comparable to the work of the mufti: do this, not that. What the mufti does is needed, otherwise the role would not exist. But it is not useful if the availability of this-or-that rulings diminishes Muslims' personal effort to know and *will* what is right.

The form of Question 2 illustrates this well: if women are commended to do the prayers in the mosque, why are they not commanded to do that, as men are? It pits one ḥadīth against another, building on a superficial inconsistency to maintain that if the commendation for women were really the same as for men, conditions around it would be the same or very similar, and they are not. But the apparent inconsistency is only perceived as such because the *sunnah* has been reduced to a ruling. The *sunnah*s as *sunnah*s cannot be definitively expressed in actionable legal language, though they can feed into such language. For example, jurists can discuss the right of wives to maintenance within or after a marriage, but they cannot, within their professional discourse, discuss the duty of mutual help, dependence, consultation, and kindness between spouses, enjoined in the Qurʾān and Sunnah for married life and for the time of divorce. The *sunnah* is that men and women are responsible for helping one another in worship by attending the prayers in a place of public assembly designated for that. If the wife of ʿUmar had not willed to preserve the *sunnah*, she might have pleased her husband by not going to the mosque for either *ʿishāʾ* or *fajr* or both prayers, but she did not. If he had not willed to preserve the *sunnah*, he would have forbidden her to go, but he did not. If ʿĀʾishah had not willed to preserve the *sunnah* she would have stopped the women guilty of the 'new thing' she disliked from going to the mosque, but she did not do even that.

The will to adhere to the Sunnah grows from a deeper root than the will to follow the rulings of *fiqh*. These rulings do have a role in educating the will: once accepted as socially approved customs they shape the environment in which are formed our likes and dislikes, our ideas of what is right and wrong. But their deeper, religious value is conditional upon their serving the relevant *sunnah*s. As we have seen in the discussion of this topic by Ibn Ḥazm, the jurists' rulings do not always do this. Those rulings lean far less on this *sunnah* than on the need to preserve social order by deterring men and women from frequenting the mosques together with mixed motives or the wrong motives. In preserving social order in this way they seek to preserve the mosques, and the motives of the men and women attending, from improper distraction. They end up doing this by making neighbourhood mosques, for all practical purposes, places for only men. For, in reality, even if women are present in these mosques, they are expected to be invisible and inaudible. That is a world away from the report we cited of a woman challenging the caliph while he was speaking his sermon, and his answer: "the woman is right." In our world, the question would not be whether the women was right, but whether she should have been attending the Friday prayer at all and, if so, whether she should have interrupted the sermon – that is, whether she should have a religious opinion that might be confidently aired in a public setting. Under the rule of the Prophet and of his Companions after him, Muslim men and women were not constrained from places where they would normally encounter each other, such as markets or mosques, but they were constrained by divine command to "lower their gaze", i.e., to avoid opportunities to flirt. During that period men did fail to obey that command, and such failure had to be dealt with. It was not then considered wise to close off all avenues that might lead to such failure, because doing so would also risk closing off the opportunities for success, beginning with the effort of patience and self-control that men and women must exercise (and exercise habitually) in order to obey the command to "lower their gaze". Just as importantly, keeping women away from the mosques reduces their own sense of the value of their concern and commitment to the institution of congregational prayer.

The cultural meanings behind legal rulings carry beyond the situations to which they are formally addressed. The diminution of an important *sunnah*, even if the diminution is the lightest form of *bidʿah* and done with the best of motives, is bound to have negative consequences. The obligatory prayers are the conspicuous symbol of being and behaving as a Muslim, an affirmation and reinforcement of the ethos of the community. If women are denied the 'right' to pray in the mosques and thereby make a contribution to the public life of Muslims – a 'right' that in theory could not be denied to male slaves, but could be denied to their female owners – this will flow over to other aspects of the status of women in other contexts. Depriving women of their public duty and dignity as Muslims, apparently with religious sanction and therefore believed and accepted, impacts the expectations society has of them. This in turn affects *all* the provisions made for them (in education, opportunities to work and travel, etc.), not just facilities in the mosques. It is bound also to impact their expectations of themselves as believers. Perhaps that is why, for many centuries up to the beginnings of the modern period, so many of the learned masters of *ḥadīth* and *fiqh*, took great pains to educate their daughters and wives in the religion. A considerable number of these women became famous scholars with prestigious teaching posts in the great metropolitan mosques and madrasas. Even within its limitations, this effort, of the men and the women, was from nearness to the *sunnah*.

Companions of God's Messenger, upon him be peace, like Ḥanzalah and Abū Bakr al-Ṣiddīq, affirm that in nearness to him the hereafter became a vivid, present reality before them, only to fade when, out of his company, everyday concerns intervened.[1] The marks of prophethood include an awareness of the Hour that is constant, undiluted and undimmed. There is confirmation from the Prophet himself, as reported by Jābir:

> Whenever God's Messenger, upon him be peace, addressed the people, his eyes would redden, and his voice rise, and his anger intensify to the point that he was like the warning-crier of an armed troop, saying, the raid is coming upon you in the morning or evening (so make ready)! He would say: "I and the Hour have been sent (as close together) as these two fingers" – and he joined his index and middle fingers (...).[2]

If the urgency of striving for the Sunnah is understood, it becomes easier to imagine the distressed rage of ʿAbdullāh ibn ʿUmar when his son Bilāl defied the command of the Prophet not to stop women going to the mosques for the prayers when that is their intention in going out. Bilāl's was a willed resolve to ignore a command of the new religion in favour of the old convention – that husbands must have, assert and display, full control of the persons and properties of their

---

1 Muslim, *Ṣaḥīḥ*, *Tawbah*, b. *faḍl dawām al-dhikr wa-l-fikr fī umūr al-ākhirah.*

2 Muslim, *Ṣaḥīḥ*, *Jumūʿah*, b. *takhfīf al-ṣalāh wa-l-khuṭbah.* See also: al-Nasāʾī, *Sunan*, k. *Ṣalāt al-ʿīdayn*, b. *kayfa al-khuṭbah*; Ibn Mājah, *Sunan*, *al-Muqaddimah*, b. *ijtināb al-bidʿah wa-l-jadal.*

wives, effectively denying them independent being. But it is that independence of being, most real in the consciousness of one's interior selfhood, that is the basis both of every person's singular individuality – which every person will carry, alone, to God, fearing His judgement and needing His mercy – and the basis in this present life, despite all its inequalities and injustices, of equality before God and hope in Him.

Bilāl's wording implies that he has high confidence that, in this matter, the old convention will prevail over the new religion. If he could have sensed, as his father sensed for him, the nearness of the Fire, he could not have said what he said. But he did not. Suppose that by some (hard to imagine) legal arrangement he might be compelled to let his wife go to the mosque for the prayers. What is there to prevent him making her life difficult in many other ways until she 'volunteers' to stop going? Nothing, except his recognition within himself that it is the women's right/obligation, by command of God's Messenger, that they should, if they can, do the prayers in the mosques. Nor can he know the benefits to himself of that recognition until after he has lived with it. The act of will to accept change must come first, but, to achieve the desired end, it must be accompanied by remorse for wrongs done and a change of heart and of mind.

The need to effect a change of heart is the reason, deeper than using the appropriate tactics (Question 6), for speaking up unequivocally for reform in conformity with the known, soundly established *sunnah* on this matter. The same need should inspire us never to urge that reform otherwise than with gentle speech, and to keep at it with as much patience as it takes to be listened to. That way of approaching the need for reform – quite at odds with the selfish impatience of contemporary habits of demand and consumption, epitomised in fast food and instant coffee – is itself a *sunnah.* Thereafter, if the desired reform takes hold, and women are accorded the dignity due to them, whether it is in the marketplace or workplace, the school campus or the mosque, or even, in some circumstances in the privacy of family homes, we have to be mindful of another (and, for the young especially, most difficult) *sunnah.* This *sunnah* is supported by an explicit divine command but its virtue and social benefits cannot be realised merely by giving it external legal definition as a right or obligation. It is the virtue that God enjoins by commanding His Messenger to command the believers, men and women alike, to "lower their gaze". Everyone readily understands that if *ḥijāb* is practised in the manner of an external conformity, a fashion accessory or identity marker, the legal demands of the ruling may appear to be met, but the meaning and purpose of the effort are not achieved. Then, *ḥijāb* is a bit of a nuisance, reluctantly or cheerfully put up with, perhaps preventing some harms, but not enabling the good of safe, civil, respectful interactions between men and women where these are normal and necessary. In the same way, if the *sunnah* we have been discussing is respected to the extent that women are permitted to pray in the mosques, and that the necessary facilities are provided for them along with (typically) a curtained-off or otherwise separated space, we must accept this with good grace as change in the right direction. But the *sunnah* is still some distance away if women are by convention more or less invisible and inaudible in the mosque. The *sunnah* is achieved for women when they can directly see and hear the imām and when, if he is speaking about and for the religion, they can speak out in order to correct any error or misguidance in what he has said. The *sunnah* is achieved for men if the imām can hear the correction and then not hesitate to say, if it is true to say, that "the woman is right".

Having made that as clear as I can, without (I hope) lapsing into the fashionable idiom of women's 'rights', it is my duty to remind readers, again as clearly as possible, that the *sunnah* has boundaries. These boundaries may not be transgressed except for some unavoidable need, and then only for the duration of that need. They certainly should not be transgressed for the sake of the popularity that is easily won by conforming to non-Muslim tastes and conventions. There is good in doing what the *sunnah* commends us to do; there is good in not-doing what it commends us not-to-do. The *sunnah* is far from being fully implemented – rather, it is being rejected and perverted – if the believers (men or women or both together) take the view that, when men and women are praying together, it does not matter how the rows are arranged or where men and women stand. The *sunnah* is being rejected and perverted if the believers take the view that it does not matter if a man or woman is leading the prayer or taking responsibility for the regular Friday sermon. In the very unlikely, not impossible situation that no competent man is available a competent woman must serve as imām – being female is not of itself a disqualification for the functions of leading the prayer or formal preaching. But this adjustment to atypical circumstance cannot be established as the normal, regular practice, nor accorded the dignity of an 'interpretation' (some species of 'non-literal conformity with the non-manifest intent') of the *sunnah*. The full explanation for this is long and must await the separate study dedicated to it.

List of works cited

Abū Dāwūd, Sulaymān ibn al-Ashʿath (d. 275/889), *al-Sunan*. Ed. Muḥammad ʿAbd al-ʿAzīz al-Khālidī. Beirut: Dār al-Kutub al-ʿIlmiyyah, 1416/1996.

Abū Nuʿaym al-Aṣbahānī (d. 430/1038), *Maʿrifat al-ṣaḥābah*. Beirut: Dār al-Kutub al-ʿIlmiyyah, 5 vols., 1422 AH.

Aḥmad ibn Ḥanbal (d. 241/855), *al-Musnad*. Cairo: al-Maṭbaʿah al-Maymaniyyah, 1313. Cairo: Maṭbaʿat al-Maʿārif, 1365 AH.

al-Bayhaqī, Abū Bakr Aḥmad ibn al-Ḥasan (d. 458/1066), *al-Sunan al-kubrā*. Ed. Muḥammad ʿAbd al-Qādir ʿAṭā. Beirut: Dār al-Kutub al-ʿIlmiyyah, 1414/1994.

al-Bukhārī, Muḥammad ibn Ismāʿīl (d. 256/870), *al-Jāmiʿ al-ṣaḥīḥ*, with its commentary by Ibn Ḥajar, *Fatḥ al-bārī*. Beirut: Dār al-Kutub al-ʿIlmiyyah, 1410/1989.

al-Dāraquṭnī, Abū al-Ḥasan ʿAlī ibn ʿUmar (d. 385/995), *al-ʿIlal al-wāridah fī al-aḥādīth al-nabawiyyah*. Ed. Maḥfūẓ al-Raḥmān Zaynullāh al-Salafī. Riyadh: Dār Ṭaybah, 1405/1985.

al-Dhahabī, Shams al-Dīn Muḥammad ibn Aḥmad (d. 748/1348), *Siyar aʿlām al-nubalāʾ*. Beirut: Muʾassasat al-Risālah, 25 vols., 1413/1993.

Taʾrīkh al-Islām. Ed. ʿUmar ʿAbd al-Salām Tadmurī. N.p.: Dār al-Kitāb al-ʿArabī, 52 vols., 1410/1990.

Tadhkirat al-ḥuffāẓ. Beirut: Dār Iḥyāʾ al-Turāth al-ʿArabī, 4 vols., n.d.

Ibn ʿAbd al-Barr, Abū ʿUmar Yūsuf ibn ʿAbdillāh al-Andalūsī (d. 463), *al-Istidhkār al-jāmiʿ li-madhāhib fuqahāʾ al-amṣār*. Damascus/ Beirut: Dār Qutaybah, 30 vols., 1414/1993..

Ibn Abī Shaybah, Abū Bakr ʿAbdullāh ibn Muḥammad (d. 235), *al-Muṣannaf*. Ed. Muḥammad ʿAwwāmah. Jeddah, Dār al-Qiblah, 1427/2006.

Ibn Ḥajar, Shihāb al-Dīn Aḥmad ibn ʿAlī al-ʿAsqalānī (d. 852/1449), *Lisān al-mīzān*. Hyderabad: Dāʾirat al-Maʿārif, 1329–31 AH.

Ibn Ḥazm, Abū Muḥammad, ʿAlī ibn Aḥmad al-Ẓāhirī al-Andalusī (d. 456/1064), *al-Muḥallā fī sharḥ al-Mujallā bi-l-ḥujaj wa-l-āthār*. Ed. Aḥmad Shākir. Cairo: al-Maṭbaʿah al-Munīriyyah, 1352 AH.

Ibn Khallikān, Shams al-Dīn Aḥmad ibn Muḥammad (d. 681/1282), *Wafayāt al-aʿyān*. Ed. Iḥsān ʿAbbās. Beirut: Dār Ṣādir, 1972.

al-Kattānī, Muḥammad al-Muntaṣir (d. 1419), *Muʿjam fiqh al-salaf*. Beirut: Dār al-Kutub al-ʿIlmiyyah, 5 vols., 2013.

Ibn Mājah, Muḥammad ibn Yazīd al-Qazwīnī (d. 273/889), *al-Sunan*. Ed. Maḥmūd Naṣṣār. Beirut: Dār al-Kutub al-ʿIlmiyyah, 1419/1998.

Ibn Qudāmah (d. 683/1223), *al-Mughnī*. Cairo: Dār al-Ḥadīth, 1416/1996.

al-Kāsānī, Abū Bakr ibn Masʿūd (d. 587/1191), *Badāʾiʿ al-ṣanāʾiʿ*. Ed. al-Shaykh ʿAlī Muḥammad Muʿawwid and al-Shaykh ʿĀdil Aḥmad al-Mawjūd. Beirut: Dār al-Kutub al-ʿIlmiyyah, 1418/1997.

Mālik ibn Anas (d. 179/795), *al-Muwaṭṭā*, narration of Yaḥyā ibn Yaḥyā al-Laythī. Beirut: n.p., 1425/2004.

al-Marghīnānī, Burhān al-Dīn Abū al-Ḥasan ʿAlī ibn Abī Bakr (d. 593/ 1197), *al-Hidāyah*. Karachi: Maktabat al-Bushrā,

1428/2007.
al-Mizzī, Abū l-Ḥajjāj Yūsuf (d. 742/1342), *Tahdhīb al-kamāl*. Ed. Bashshār ᶜAwwād Maᶜrūf. Beirut: Muʾassasat al-Risālah, 35 vols., 1406/1985.
Muḥammad Abū Zahrah (d. 1394/1974), *Ibn Ḥazm ḥayātuhū wa-ᶜaṣruhū fiqhuhū wa-ārāʾuhū*. Cairo: Dār al-Fikr al-ᶜArabī, 1954.
Muslim ibn al-Ḥajjāj al-Naysābūrī (d. 261/874-5), *al-Jāmiᶜ al-ṣaḥīḥ*, with the commentary by al-Nawawī. Beirut: Dār al-Kutub al-ᶜIlmiyyah. 1415/1995.
al-Nasaʾī, ᶜAbd al-Raḥmān ibn Aḥmad ibn Shuᶜayb (d. 303/ 915): *al-Mujtabā*. Beirut: Dār al-Kutub al-ᶜIlmiyyah. 1416/1995.
Saᶜīd ibn Manṣūr (d. 227/841), *al-Sunan*. Ed. Ḥabīb al-Raḥmān al-Aᶜẓamī. India: al-Dār al-Salafiyyah, 1403/1982.
al-Ṣanᶜānī, ᶜAbd al-Razzāq ibn Hammām (d. 211/826), *al-Muṣannaf*. Ed. Ḥabīb al-Raḥmān al-Aᶜẓamī. Beirut: al-Maktab al-Islāmī, 2nd edn., 1403/1983.
al-Shaybānī, Muḥammad ibn al-Ḥasan (d. 189/805), *K. al-Ḥujjah ᶜalā ahl al-madīnah*. Beirut: ᶜĀlam al-Kutub, 1427/2006.
Kitāb al-Aṣl. Beirut: Dār Ibn Ḥazm, 13 vols., 1433/2012
al-Tirmidhī, Muḥammad ibn ᶜĪsā (d. 279/892), *al-Sunan*. Ed. Aḥmad Shākir. Beirut: Dār Iḥyāʾ al-Turāth al-ᶜArabī, 1415/1995.